GONE

The Disappearance of Community in the Modern American Church

BRUCE SNOAP

WESTBOW
PRESS
A DIVISION OF THOMAS NELSON

WestBow Press books may be ordered through booksellers or by contacting:

WestBow Press
A Division of Thomas Nelson
1663 Liberty Drive
Bloomington, IN 47403
www.westbowpress.com
1-(866) 928-1240

Because of the dynamic nature of the Internet, any web addresses or links contained in this book may have changed since publication and may no longer be valid. The views expressed in this work are solely those of the author and do not necessarily reflect the views of the publisher, and the publisher hereby disclaims any responsibility for them.

Any people depicted in stock imagery provided by Thinkstock are models, and such images are being used for illustrative purposes only.
Certain stock imagery © Thinkstock.

Cover Design by: Jeff Grooters

ISBN: 978-1-4497-5604-8 (hc)
ISBN: 978-1-4497-5603-1 (sc)
ISBN: 978-1-4497-5602-4 (e)

Library of Congress Control Number: 2012910305

Printed in the United States of America

WestBow Press rev. date: 09/25/2012

Contents

To Dr. Wayne G. Boulton and Dr. Steven Bridge, who taught me about community and the call of Christ.

To Sam, Mac, Belle, Annie, and Ian.

CHAPTER 1

A Land of Togetherness in a Sea of Isolation

We are family,
get up everybody and sing
—Sister Sledge

I have found that the Lord takes us on varying adventures throughout our lives. Sometimes they are small; sometimes they are life-changing. But what I have always found is that when the Lord calls, we are missing out if we do not follow.

Over the past few years the Lord has been leading me into a new, albeit very old, way of gathering and living. Any Rev. Ray Vander Laan devotees will be familiar with the word *insula*. Let me explain that insula is the direction in which the Lord has been leading me. This Latin word means "apartment" or "communal living." In a faith sense it is community, each of us living in community with others the Lord brings into our lives. It is knowing and being known; it is living, loving, and sharing all the joys and burdens this life provides. It is walking together in Christ's path so each day we are more like him.

Moderation in Everything—Or at Least in the Things that May Affect My Life

The world seems to have convinced us individually and collectively that as we strive for the life of Christ we should temper our walk of faith, making sure our worldly obligations and desires are not neglected for the sake of radical faith.

"Moderation in everything" seems to be a Christian mantra in most twenty-first-century American churches. But I have come to believe that following Jesus in moderation is not an option. This by no means that we are to sell everything, buy a big, abandoned building, and begin living together to "follow *Jeeeeessssssuuussssss.*"

Times and cultures change. While we may not employ the same methods or customs the church in Jerusalem did, we should live with the spirit and the desire those people had, especially as they are depicted in the book of Acts, just after Jesus ascended to heaven.

We have all been called by God to different lives. In our culture we could not easily sell our possessions and move in with others in a big building, but this does not mean we ignore the principles and spirit of the first church. Having all things in common does not have to mean we all live the same life in the same house. It should mean, however, that we are close enough and in contact enough with each other that we know everything about each other. We are closer than family. We are an insula.

An insula is not family in the same sense we usually define family; it is not a parent you love, a brother you tolerate, or an uncle you keep your kids away from. An insula is the family of God. We have different homes, spouses, and jobs. In some ways our lives should never connect, but because of Christ they are all intricately interwoven.

What I believe God is beginning here is not a new thing, nor is it a twelve-step program we can get involved in for a little while and then get back to normal. An insula should be an integral part of our lives as we move forward with the people God has brought together to seek him and his will first. It is a group of individuals walking the same path in community with God and with those he has brought around us. It is family.

As you can imagine, this is no small commitment; it is a call to radically change from twenty-first-century American living to Christ living.

This is not an Essene movement; it is a Christ movement. It is not a new denomination or church; it is a Christ calling. It is simply discipleship as God desires us to do. It is a call from God, and as with any true call from God, if you begin to walk it, your life will never be the same.

In the Gospel of Matthew, Jesus walked by the Sea of Galilee. He called Peter and Andrew, then James and John, and they followed immediately. I believe I am being called, and I can't help but want to take steps in that direction, but this is not to suggest you have been called and should follow. The reason I am writing to you is because I have no doubt if God calls you, you'll follow.

As an insula—as in our whole lives—God does not call us alone. We are to go in community. I have a desire to be in community, in an insula. Is God calling you to an insula?

The Calling and the Cost

Is God calling you to become part of an insula? Is God calling you to go beyond church conventions or Bible study at the Johnson's? Is God calling you to step out in faith and become more than you thought was possible in this American life?

When will we walk the walk of faith so it actually costs something? When will we go forward despite conventional wisdom and acknowledge that God's wisdom is quite different from our own and that God's actions are not ours? Only in beginning to look at life and faith in global and ancestral contexts, using local and long-term views, can we break the chains of society and culture that bind us daily. Only when we break through the wisdom that considers it absurd to believe that the Bible is literal and that we did not descend from a primordial soup will we be able to begin to walk in true obedience to God.

America is one of the few countries where this is possible. While our culture and society have pulled us away from following God, it is that same culture and society we've been blessed to live in that allow us the opportunity to break our bond and pursue God without human limits.

In my life I have fought groups. I grew up in the 1970s, when one of the most popular commercials was for a soft drink; a cornucopia of singers wishing to teach the world to sing held the soft drink while enjoying the bliss of "togetherness." My life around the adults of the 1960s and 1970s was one of peace in and love out. We were one groovy group that fought "the man" by banding together and discovering what life truly meant.

In my rebellion as an adult I have fought togetherness, I have fought groups, I have fought being "one of the guys," and I have fought being part of a community. God has much more endurance than I do. God created humanity to be together.

After the Beginning

The first chapter of Genesis says, "Then God said, 'Let us make man in our image, in our likeness . . . So God created mankind in his own image, in the image of God he created them; male and female he created them' (Genesis 1:26-27 NIV84).

Genesis 2 of course goes into greater detail about the creation of Adam and Eve and gives a more expanded story of the world's creation. But in the two verses I cited, he created male and female at the same time. He created us to need each other, to be in community together, to walk alongside of and occasionally carry each other.

God calls us to community in Genesis 2. After God had created everything, and Adam had started working in the garden, God looked down and said, "It is not good for man to be alone" (Genesis 2:18). What I didn't realize for a long time was that Adam had not been alone; God had been with him, but he knew he wasn't enough for Adam. He knew that human beings could never completely connect to him the way he wanted and that we would need other people to fulfill the true purpose of our lives.

God himself is a community; God states, "Let us . . ." *Us?* This is *God!* How can there be an *us?* But from the beginning, God's Trinity was in community with itself. As John 1:1-2 says, "In the beginning was the Word, and the Word was with God, and the Word was God. He was with God in the beginning."

From the beginning there was community. From the beginning there was an us, and we are to carry on that practice. We are not to be alone in our walk with Christ, and in that light we need to seek others to walk alongside us in our pursuit of Christ. We walk with each other as we go to weekly worship services, but there is very little community in those services. Typically we are in a group numbering between 150 and 1,200. One church not far from my town has weekly services for 10,000. How can community happen there?

You know some of those with you in the pews, you recognize many others, but you know very few intimately. You don't know who's having difficulty in his or her marriage or has children wandering down dangerous paths or is drinking too much or dabbling in Internet porn. Nor do any of those people you meet with on Sunday know any of these things about you. They know if you have health issues only if you're listed in the bulletin. They may know you are going through a divorce if you and your spouse got into a very public fight about who gets to stay in current relationships—including those at church. They don't know if you feel like you can't take another step and don't care about that. They can see you and say hi without ever realizing your son has just stolen your stereo to raise some money for drugs. They can see you without realizing you and the woman three rows in front have been having an affair for three months now.

Sunday is about Sunday; the rest of the week—the rest of life—rarely invades the sanctity and the serenity Sunday offers. But an insula is not supposed to replace Sunday corporate worship. An insula is not to take the place of communally worshiping the God of the universe with other believers. A group of believers gathered to discern the will of God is a church; otherwise, it's a group of people who have great meals, great laughter, and a burning desire to be more like the Father.

Inheritance Leeches

Dietrich Bonhoeffer speaks of cheap grace versus costly grace in his book *The Cost of Discipleship*. We as an American Church—and specifically I—have relied much too often on this cheap grace. Grace by most popular definitions is getting what we don't deserve. I have gladly accepted the blessings of God without realizing how much I falter in my walk of faith. I have taken the inheritance of blessing freely given by God and sucked all the marrow I could from it. I still want more. I gladly take the good things God gives me and sometimes give a polite thank you. I don't realize the cost of the grace I've received; I see grace as the good things that come my way. I don't call it grace when I get hardships and suffering I don't deserve. Grace seems to apply only to the good things I get. But that is our society, not the Bible, speaking.

Job did not deserve any of the things God allowed Satan to afflict him with, but God's grace was there even in Job's suffering.

If we go through a tremendous difficulty and grow and learn from it and end up wiser, more able to help people, and closer to God even though it was painful and hard, isn't that grace God has given us? But in America we cannot fathom something that hurts being grace-filled. We have gotten our cake and are eating away without concern or care for those around us.

We have seen the prayer of Jabez and declared it as a right for anyone who is willing to repeat his words. But we miss quite a bit, and as Americans it never occurs to us to analyze the verse before the prayer. Jabez's prayer takes place in 1 Chronicles 4:10, so as good Americans we start there. We read the prayer, see that God answered his prayer, and then we shout "Praise the Lord! I want that too!" and go on as if we deserved the same thing as Jabez and think God has to give it to us.

But verse 9 states that Jabez was more honorable than his brothers. The implication is that Jabez was a man of integrity and honor not just in his immediate family but also within the greater community. How many people who have prayed the prayer of Jabez were righteous people in their communities? How many people who have prayed the prayer of Jabez were the most honored in their families, families not filled with lowlifes and drug dealers but with other very exemplary people?

We don't want to work at being the most honored; we simply want God to answer our prayers and bless us, increase our territory, and keep us free from pain. Isn't that the American dream? A lot of property and money and no pain? That's what we all pray and strive for to lesser or greater degrees, but very few of us are the most honored people in our communities or are willing to work at becoming the righteous type of individual who deserves such a blessing.

Cultural Divide

I look at the world and wonder if I can escape the culture I was born into. Many people don't think they can. Some Muslim extremists would cut off my head if they had the chance just because I was born in this culture. Some white supremacists in this country would shoot me or hang me because I believe in the words of Martin Luther King, Jr. when he said in his "I have a dream" speech that people should be judged not by the color of their skin but by the content of their character. Some people think no one can truly worship God in song except with words directly from the Book of Psalms and accompanied by the organ, and anyone who adds words or instruments is disobeying and destined for hell.

These are all today's realities of living in this world, a world of intolerance, a world of the "get-mine" syndrome. You have the right to believe in anything you want in this world unless it's the saving grace of Jesus Christ; if you do, you're an intolerant bigot who needs to be eliminated from this enlightened, tolerant society.

We live in a society that sees no correlation between violence in movies and real life even though video-game sales and crime statistics steadily rise. This society claims pornography has no ill effects even though its divorce rate has risen to 58 percent (www.divorcerate.org). It holds the renaissance of humanity as its highest value while people all over the world are murdered because they are different or just in the way. We have declared, "The King [God] is dead; long live the King [humanity]!" We believe we are the height of civilization, just as the ancient Greeks did. Humanity is the apex of evolution and can learn everything.

Yet interestingly, in our American culture, we secretly do not believe we are the end of all things. In a 2004 poll by CBS (www.cbsnews.com/stories/2004/11/22/opinion/polls/main657083.shtm), 55 percent of Americans believe humanity was created in its current form by God. You would never know that by attending our universities or by watching our media. If you follow their lines of thought, only an idiot would believe God created people thousands of years ago, but in large part that's because if we acknowledge the existence of a creator, we are responsible to that creator. If we acknowledge the existence of God, then we have to at least pay a little attention to what he wants and how he wants us to live. But we don't want anything to do with that; we're going to want what we want the way we want. We are going to have sex with those we want when we want. We are going to eat and drink and smoke what we want when we want. We are in charge of our lives, and no one is going to tell us what we have to do.

This is a path I can no longer stay on. Pulling myself up by my bootstraps gets me only deeper in the quicksand of this world.

Toto Finally Pulled Back Our Curtain

The Apostle Paul writes we cannot hold Gentiles—unbelievers—to the law because they do not know the law, but once the law is made known to them, they—we—are without excuse. I have been shown my false path of discipleship, and now that I know that, I must step onto the road less traveled and follow him.

Once something has been revealed to us, we are obliged to take action. Once the truth has been made known to us, we cannot journey down the path we had been walking on previously. Once we realize the American way of life is not God's way of life, how can we proceed as if that truth has not been revealed to us? The American way of life is not worthless; quite the contrary the American way of life is probably the best way humanity can live life apart from God. Note the key words: "apart from God." Without God we have developed a system that is basically fair and honorable. Even as I write that statement, one of my seminary professors is screaming in my mind that my premise of creating something good without God is one of the largest errors I have ever made.

We can't do anything good without the influence of God. Apart from God, all is ruin; apart from God, all is sin. But with God's gift of free will, not only do we have the freedom to do as we please regardless of God's wishes, we actually have the freedom to deny there is a God. We have the freedom to rely on our wisdom and our logic to run our lives. But even more insidious is that we have the freedom to praise God on Sunday and then on Tuesday completely ignore his word, his call, his love, only to have the freedom to come back on Sunday and ask forgiveness for the sins we committed during the week and go out and commit them all over again. We Christians have been shown a better way of life, a better way of being in relationship with God and with each other.

In our wisdom we have decided it is not possible to be like the first-century church, and so we have stopped trying. We have acknowledged we don't have all the answers, and so rather than default to the God who does have the answers we have picked over the answers the world has given us and grabbed for ourselves those that least offend us.

We are not, to use that Seinfeld idiom, "kings of our castle" although we live as if we are. We are simply resident aliens living in a created, fallen world. We are to be in the world but not of the world. We are to go into the world not to fit in and make a dwelling place but to bring back others with whom God would like to have a relationship as well. We are to be family with those God brings into our lives. We are to be an insula.

CHAPTER 2

Institutionalization:
It's Not All It's Cracked Up to Be

and try as you may, there isn't a way
to explain the kind of change
that would make an Eskimo renounce fur
that would make a vegetarian barbecue hamster

—Steve Taylor

From time to time God will lead us to where we do not know; lately, God has been leading me in a direction I did not anticipate. He seems to be moving through some people I've been talking with. I've been asked to walk specifically in community with a select group of people and with Christ. Like Abraham, I have been called but have no idea where we will end up or what it will look like, but I do feel this is a call from God and the right path to take.

For me and apparently some others, the institutionalized church is not walking the same path as Christ. Many institutional churches are doing wonderful and amazing things, and each church has its own personality and agenda. I do not wish to cut down or degrade their works, but the people who make up the church, not the institution itself, are the bride of Christ.

Most church leaders are there because they went to seminary, passed a test, and convinced some people to let them be part of the vocational church. In today's institutional church there is a bit of a disparity for people who feel called to be pastors in that they don't have to be called by God, they don't have to be gifted, and they don't have to be the one with authority. To be part of a ministry and to assure quality of training, they simply have to be ordained.

Ordination is not a biblical criterion for leading people into the kingdom of God; it is an institutional creation that helps those who want to be pastors. Two of the godliest men I have ever had the privilege to call friends have graduated from seminary but had to jump through quite a few ordination hoops or the seminary would not "certify" them. One of them is not only a rabid Bears and Bulls fan, he is a biblical encyclopedia. He knows more about the Bible, where to find things in the text and how it all relates to our lives than anyone I have met. He can preach; he has the most generous, kind spirit I have ever known, but he still had to jump through hoops or be kept from the ministry because his seminary professors didn't like his conservative philosophy. Ordination can be a stepping-stone that assures quality leadership; it can also be a way of enforcing certain criteria and codes of uniformity regardless of the person's convictions or spiritual gifts.

Quite often I heard graduating seminarians say, "Just say what you know they want to hear so you can get ordained; then you can do the right thing once you're in a church." Still other students are allowed to sail through seminary in spite of the fact they have no real spiritual gifts or authority that make them people who should be in charge of God's kingdom; they simply knew what hoops to jump through. They say they have hearts that wish to do what they believe God has called them to, but they also have a desire to lead, to be in authority. They seem to have been called by their own ambition and by the institution rather than by God. We all have encountered people who are pastors because they could not lead anywhere else, and a congregation's capacity for grace is greater than anywhere else in the world.

We are not called to build the church; that's God's job. We are not called to set up institutional standards that qualify people to lead; that's also God's job. We are simply called to make disciples.

The Liar Within Us All

Recently I listened to a CD of a worship conference at which Rev. Ray Vander Laan was the speaker. He said a Jewish rabbi who spoke at a conference he'd attended said that Christians who claimed to be disciples of Christ but did not read the four Gospels at least once a month were liars. I don't know if Rev. Vander Laan or any other Christian teacher agrees with that, and at first I thought the rabbi was full of it, but the more I let those words soak in, the more I realized the rabbi was absolutely correct. A disciple is not simply someone who knows Jesus is the son of God and died for our sins; demons know this, but they aren't disciples. A disciple is someone who knows Jesus and with every fiber of his or her being wants to be just like Jesus.

Without direct, divine intercession, the only way to know the Messiah is to know the text. I have been through Sunday school, religious college, and seminary, and today I learned that Jesus was healing people and possibly raising the dead according to Luke before he called one disciple. He was ministering to the people and bringing the message of the kingdom of God before he called one disciple. This doesn't change one thing about my belief in Jesus; it doesn't change one miracle he performed or one word he said. But how could I have missed that after all the religion classes and all the Bible study? How many other things that tell me about the rabbi I am trying to follow have I missed? How much do I really know about this Jesus?

Not one professor I have ever had, not one group I was ever in talked about Jesus having a sense of humor, but in the book of Mark, when Jesus watched his disciples rowing across the Sea of Galilee all night (Mark 6:45-56), he went out to them. This is one version of the story of Jesus walking on water, a story Christians have heard in their first Sunday school lessons; a story most of us could tell in our sleep. It's a story that shows the true humor of Jesus. Matthew and John tell the story also, but if you read only their versions you don't see Jesus' humor. In Mark's version Jesus is walking toward the disciples, who are struggling to row against the night wind. Mark lets us know that Jesus was just about to walk *past* the boat when the disciples saw him and thought he was a ghost. He had to stop to calm them.

If you read only some of the Gospels you would have missed knowing Jesus in this way. He didn't come out to show them the mighty miracle of walking on water; he didn't come out to save them from drowning. He was walking past them to get to the other side first. He was playing a practical joke on them.

You have every right to disagree with me. But isn't the only reason you'd walk past your friends struggling in a boat so you could smile as they came ashore and ask them, "What took you so long?"

Jesus had a sense of humor. Jesus liked the young men who were his disciples. Jesus loved the community he was with, and he showed it in all the ways we do today. We are serious, sorrowful, theological, logical, and just like Jesus we are humorous.

Unless we truly know the text we can't know Jesus, and if we can't know Jesus apart from the text, how can we think we'll be able to develop a true community without the text?

There are people in an insula who rise to the surface; not just one person will lead. God is calling a community of committed believers together with Jesus Christ as the head, and each of us is part of the priesthood of believers sharing, teaching, and learning together. While I am more likely than some to have an opinion about the text—my bride is rolling her eyes right now, knowing I always have an opinion—and I am eager to share that opinion, it in no way means I am a person with God's insight and wisdom. Only collectively can we truly see God's wisdom, and only through sharing our views and experiences can we get a better—albeit still dim—picture of what God is calling and doing in this world.

We are called to the words of Matthew, who quoted Jesus saying, "All authority in heaven and on earth has been given to me. Go therefore and make disciples of all nations, baptizing them in the name of the Father and of the Son and of the Holy Spirit, and teaching them to obey everything that I have commanded you" (Matthew 28:18-19).

It Is Not

While some wonderful churches are doing amazing things, I have not found one in which disciple making is its main focus and action. We are so caught up in programs, outreaches, evangelism, and meeting the needs brought before the senior pastor or consistory ("council," for you vineyard folks) that we assume discipleship is happening in those activities. It is not.

The biblical literacy rate in today's American culture is astonishingly low. Instead of investing our lives in a few people, we hand out as many tracts as possible and feel good about that. Instead of returning each year to the same place to serve the same people and develop lasting relationships, we seek new places and new opportunities so we won't get bored with "mission work." Instead of truly diving into the text with a small group of the same people for a long time, we either develop a very superficial, cliquish group or get deep for about twelve weeks and then feel we have to move on so we don't become stiff-necked and complacent.

When I was at seminary, I asked at least dozens of students and pastors to name all sixty-six of the Bible's books from memory; none could do it. You may think that remembering the books is insignificant, but if we can't remember sixty-six names, how are you ever going to "hide your word in my heart that I might not sin against you" (Psalm 119:11)?

It must begin with remembering the text. I have found very few people who can really live out the text in solitude. We can gain insight and wisdom, even a direction and a calling, in solitude, but the act of remembering in our hearts and applying the Word of God to our lives is a communal act bantered around and bounced back and forth with other people who are living a text-filled life.

Throughout the Scriptures Jesus constantly refers to the Old Testament. Many of the words he uses are not his but those of Isaiah or Zechariah or other prophets or the Torah. In an interesting twist, Jesus used the text to speak to people and answer questions. This was not original to Jesus; in traditional rabbinical arguments you argued about spiritual matters but did not give the great American prefaces, "I feel" or "I think," to defend your point of view. You quoted Scripture. Your words meant nothing in determining what God wanted from his word. It was God's words that mattered, that made the difference, not ours. What you thought was not relevant because your thinking was flawed, imperfect, and given to the whim of whatever wind was blowing that made you think you had the knowledge of God, just as mine was.

It was God's thinking that mattered, that brought us closer to his word. But in order to argue using the word of God, you had to know the word of God. You couldn't cite an opinion if you didn't know it. We, like Jesus, are to know the text so well that we don't need the reference or concordance section or a search engine to know or find Scripture. If we really know Scripture, we can see the deeper meanings to our lives and not just the surface images that give us the little bit of inspiration we need to get through the day with songs in our hearts and smiles on our faces.

I was a religion major at a Christian college; I graduated with a master's from seminary and for a long time have been researching the meanings of verses in writings and commentaries. But it was not until I was in my late thirties that I discovered a different interpretation to John the Baptist's question to Jesus whether Jesus was the Messiah when he sent his disciples to ask Jesus, "Are you the one who was to come?" (Matthew 11:2)

We spend much time on cultural sensitivity and gender sensitivity and reaching the "lost," not that they aren't important, but we don't have any time for discipleship, learning more about and becoming like Christ. We spend our time bickering about the war and about the gays in our midst that we never stop to think about simply being more like Christ. When John sent his disciples to see if Jesus was the coming one, most people, I've found, believe John doubted that Jesus was the Messiah. But the phrase "the coming one" or "the one who was to come" is part of the biblical text, part of the Old Testament, though John would not have thought of it as the Old Testament.

Zechariah 9 has a similar phrasing that foreshadows the Messiah. "The King, the one to come" is a part of the prophetic words from Zechariah regarding the Messiah. He is, in Zechariah 9:11, the one to set the prisoners free.

While there are other actions the Messiah will take, setting the prisoners free is among them. We don't know for certain whether John was asking, "Are you the Messiah?" or "Are you the one to set the prisoners free?" but Jesus' response to John is interesting. John sends a quote from the prophets of old. Jesus responds not just in his own words but also with the words of Isaiah. In Isaiah chapter 35 and then in chapter 42, the prophet describes the servant of the Lord, the Messiah to come. Isaiah states, "Be strong, do not fear; your God will come, he will come with vengeance; with divine retribution he will come to save you. Then will the eyes of the blind be opened and the ears of the deaf unstopped. Then will the lame leap like a deer, and the mute tongue shout for joy" (Isaiah 35:4-6).

Isaiah follows up the Messiah prophecy, showing that the Messiah will "open eyes that are blind, to free captives from prison and to release from the dungeon those who sit in darkness" (Isaiah 42:7). Isaiah continues: "The spirit of the sovereign Lord is on me, because the Lord has anointed me to preach good news to the poor. He has sent me to bind up the brokenhearted, to proclaim freedom for the captives and release from the darkness for the prisoners" (Isaiah 61:1).

Jesus quotes Isaiah quite often in his ministry. Just as the rabbis before and since, when he makes his point it is not an "I feel" situation. Jesus quotes from the sacred writings to convey his message. But notice what he leaves out from the prophet Isaiah passage: John asks, "Are you the coming one?" From Zechariah we know that part of the coming one's job is to set the prisoners free. When Jesus answers John, his quotes from the prophet Isaiah show he is completing the tasks of the Messiah, but he is not setting the prisoners free.

He tells John's disciples to go and report what is happening. He has reminded John that he is the Messiah, but just as important, he lets John know he is not going to get out of prison. Jesus goes on to state that there is no one greater born of woman than John the Baptist, and he just told John he was going to die in prison.

Without that understanding of the text, Jesus' words "Blessed is the man who does not fall away on account of me" (Matthew 11:6) never made any sense. Jesus seems to tell John he is doing all the things the Messiah would be doing, so why would anyone fall away because of the Messiah's miracles? But it is not until you know the text and see what Jesus left out that you realize Jesus did not just remind John he was the Messiah, he also told John he was going to die in prison. That is why John was not to lose faith; that is why John was not to fall away; he was just told he would die in prison. The prisoners were not going to be set free—yet.

Hearing that Jesus was doing the tasks the Messiah was to do would never make someone fall away on Jesus' account, but hearing that your life will not improve until you are with the Lord could easily make someone stumble and lose faith.

Without knowing the text, the whole text, we see only half the picture at best. Without knowing the text, we miss a lot of what Jesus is trying to tell us. Without knowing the text, we cannot know Jesus.

Dietrich Bonhoeffer said this of the church:

Is it really the task of the church today to offer the world solutions for its problems? Are there even Christian solutions to worldly problems? It apparently depends on what is meant by this. If one implies that Christianity has an answer to all social and political questions of the world, so that one would only have to listen to these answers to put the world in order, then this is obviously wrong. If one implies that from its vantage point Christianity has something specific to say about worldly things, then it is correct . . . . The kind of thinking that starts out with human problems and then looks for solutions from that vantage point has to be overcome—it is unbiblical. The way of Jesus Christ, and thus the way of all Christian thought, is not the way from the world to God but from God to the world. This means that the essence of the gospel does not consist in solving worldly problems, and also that this cannot be the essential task of the church. However, it does not follow from this that the church would have to task at all in this regard. But we will not recognize its legitimate task unless we first find the correct starting point. (*Ethics* 353-354, 356)

The error the institutional church commits is looking at the world and asking, "God, what can we do?" instead of looking at God and asking, "God, how can we be more like you?" and letting the world follow its lead. Our job is not to reach everyone; we may impact only a few people in our lives, but Jesus discipled twelve and that changed the world.

Discipleship, Culture, and a True Miracle

I have some idea of what discipleship is to me, but discipleship has been so ignored in America's Christian culture that I am not sure anyone really knows what true discipleship looks like nor what the results of true discipleship will bring.

As people in a specific culture, we are so desensitized by religion and so jaded by our Western mentality that we don't expect miracles—those are just in cute movies and supposed to make us feel better. For those

Christians who do see miracles, it seems the only value they place on them is as tools to reach the lost.

I've recently become aware of a true miracle in this world. Her name is Jordyn. Jordyn, who came into the world in 1988, is the first child of my best friend, and I've known her since she was a week old.

After the first of my three girls was born, I looked for female role models I could lift up so she would have people to imitate and emulate. Being the typical male, I never conceived of role models by gender; then again, I don't know I had any women role models to think about. As I began looking at this world, I discovered they were somewhat difficult to find.

There really is no one in popular culture I'm excited about lifting up. In my own life I was so unaware of great women around me I had to pause. I definitely considered my bride and my kids' godmother, Karen, along with a couple of other very inspirational, close friends to be role models, but I didn't see many more to turn to. As I looked at younger people, however, I realized that one person I have known her whole life had developed into the very definition of a biblical woman of God. Confronted with all of today's distractions, temptations, and pressures, Jordyn has managed to stay above the fray and live a truly godly life. She has continued to exceed all the expectations I had of a young person in today's world. God has used Jordyn not only to challenge and strengthen me but through her to give me hope he is still greater than the trappings of this world.

While Jordyn's off at college, she'll still be part of my insula, and we'll support, pray for, and help her in any way we can because she's family. She knows God probably better than most Christians in my life, but in most institutional churches she would go mostly unnoticed because she's not lost or any trouble at all. In a truly disciple-making community, Jordyn and others like her would be the foundation of modeling.

That is the environment I wish to be part of; that is the community I want to live in, invest in, and grow with. The beginning phase I feel led to explore is not drawing in and keeping out the world but drawing close to others and becoming equipped to reach out to the world.

If you are engaged in programs, drop-in activities, evangelizing, dramas, YWAM, and everything else, you're not making disciples. If you are truly making disciples, then you can't help but be doing some of if not all the activities I just listed.

As important as all those things are, Jesus did not say go and start a mission base, go evangelize the inner city, begin a head-start program. He simply said, "Go and make disciples." That has to be our priority, our focus.

We can live a life worthy of Christ and have an impact similar to the first apostles. If, though, we follow the path of other American churches, we will have a beautiful building and a mostly happy congregation but no disciples, no one intentionally walking in the footsteps of Christ.

How can we call ourselves disciples when we can't tell you what Jesus said about most subjects? If I can tell you what Animotion's only hit was and recite the names of all the kids on *The Brady Bunch* and *The Partridge Family* shows, if I can sing along with every song on Pink Floyd's "The Wall," but I can't recite more than five or six words of the Sermon on the Mount, how much of a disciple am I?

I can remember the specs and pricing of every product in the company I work for, but I can't tell you in which gospel Jesus proclaims himself "the light of the world." That bothered me, so I looked it up. It's John.

I crave to know the Word more and to know God. Without the text you cannot know God. One person alone can get off track in the text unless another disciple is there to verify, question, or counter.

This is what an insula should be. I've recently been made aware of a young man with amazing faith. Herbert is a man of God who is "going out" in ways I admire and support. He goes on walkabouts; he simply goes where he feels God calling no matter how remote or how dangerous this can be from a worldly standpoint.

Herbert has been used by God; he's seen God perform many miracles and is bringing the kingdom of God about in ways I haven't heard of since the first-century church. My only issue with Herbert's philosophy of ministry is that it is not practical for people with commitments. Herbert, in his early twenties, has no responsibilities besides following God's call. I am in my early forties with four kids, one dog, and a mortgage. Herbert is living on the edge in a way people with families cannot. He is self-aware enough to realize his path is not everyone's, but his quest should be ours; his mission should be ours.

How can we live radically for Christ while still honoring the commitments and obligations God has given us? This seems to be the question Herbert asks, and it becomes the test and adventure for me and others like me. Simply because we have responsibilities that preclude us from going to Africa and walking around and trusting God to provide food and shelter doesn't mean we're not to take that same love and trust of God into our own lives and live it every moment, every day.

Herbert's case reminds me we are all in very different places, and that's how a community should be. We are not coming into community to become like each other or to become ideological clones. A true community has differences and acknowledges and embraces them. We all walk at different speeds in coming to Christ; we are simply called to walk alongside each other, slowing down or speeding up occasionally as needed. We are to send out and receive back so each person can follow Christ and share in his fellowship.

When Abraham and Sarah went to the "land I will show you," they faced many obstacles and hazards on the way. Keeping Christ at the front and walking together, we can weather anything that comes along. That is an insula.

The obstacles we encounter are going to surprise us. How we stay on track and defend ourselves from those obstacles is twofold. The first is the obvious one: community. Having around you people who want God's best for you will help keep you on the right path. But just as important, if not more so, is the text. Knowing the text and thus knowing God's call for our lives is of utmost importance. If we know the text, we know how God wants us to deal with a situation. If we kind of know the text, we can make good, educated guesses and be right lots of times. If we, like me, barely know the text, we have only our wisdom to divine the correct course, and we'll be wrong most of the time.

If we know the text we can apply the text and have God's counsel with us at all times. It is in knowing the text and then following it that we can walk upright and blameless in the sight of the Lord.

Herbert and I have met only once, and that was just a "Hello, nice to meet you." I have not met Dietrich Bonhoeffer or Ray Vander Laan, but they have impacted me profoundly. How are we to live? How are we to become more like Christ? Can we explore a radical living of Christ and still live in America? Can we walk so close to Christ that the dust of his sandals falls on us?

CHAPTER 3

Deconstructing Our Understanding of Jesus

There must be some misunderstanding
There must be some kind of mistake
I waited in the rain for hours
And you were late

—Genesis

As we begin to evaluate our faith, we have to break down the things of the past to get to the root of what is truth and what has been tainted. This beginning phase of discernment is what I call "deconstructing Jesus."

To begin with, the phrase "deconstructing Jesus" might be a bit misleading. To be honest it's not Jesus we'll be taking apart but our understanding, beliefs, and views of Jesus and the Bible and faith in general.

Most of what we know in our lives we have learned from other people and our experiences. Through those teachings and experiences we have developed habits and ideologies that make up the belief system we live by. All our beliefs are given to us and heavily influenced by other people. Those "others" saw through lenses as they taught us. Just as each person is different, each lens will be different. As we get older and begin to make decisions for ourselves, we also see through the lenses of our experiences and our ideas on how life should be lived.

Even though different lenses shape us, our lenses are important, and no lens is necessarily better than another; nobody's perspective is more valid than ours when it comes to our own lives. We all have different perspectives based on our experiences and how those experiences logically fit into our lives. While your lens may not do anything for me, it is a truth for you, and I should not denigrate or belittle it; conversely, my lens does not need to change merely for the sake of yours.

The lenses people see through are all different types, but I believe they fall into three categories: modern glass, beveled glass, and stained glass. Sometimes the lenses we were taught to see through are like modern windows with minimal distortion and interference, and so we can see pretty clearly through them. Other times we were taught with lenses that resemble the beveled glass common in nineteenth-century homes. With this type of lens you can see out pretty well, but the images are a bit distorted and aren't very accurate. You get the general image and impression of what is really there, but the images are not very clear. A lot of what we learned, though, came through lenses of stained glass. Stained glass is beautiful, historical, colorful, full of imagery and meaning, and beloved. But when you look through it, you cannot see what's really out there. This doesn't lessen the possible impact or reverence one can have for such glass, but it does mean it should be viewed properly and not given the same weight as a true reflection of Christ.

Modern glass makes lenses we look through when we look at a family members or good friends. We see their good and bad points very clearly. The good is that we know who they are; the bad is that sometimes we see the bad so clearly that we can't overlook it. Certain behaviors can never be overlooked, but here I'm referring to the lesser "bad" behaviors that are not dangerous or hurtful, just annoying.

Beveled glass lenses are those most people see through when they're in midlife and looking back on their younger days. Everyone has an uncle or parent who walked twelve miles to school in the driving snow, uphill both ways, and who was just grateful to have had shoes. The good in these lenses is that there is an appreciation for the view they may not have had when they were in the middle of situations; the bad is that even though they may have had to endure snow, that snow has grown to Herculean proportions, and no one can match the grateful misery they endured.

Stained glass lenses are those people look through most commonly when they are viewing meaningful, significant history. The 1950s has been immortalized in stained glass through television shows such as *Leave It to Beaver* and *Ozzie and Harriet* that depicted a "perfect" time, but if we take a modern glass look at the 1950s, we see they were quite a bit like other decades, with good times and not-so-great times. Think about segregated drinking fountains.

Stained glass is not just a metaphor; it has practical applications of not seeing clearly also. Most stained glass windows in churches depict Jesus and the disciples as older men either balding or with white hair. But all evidence of Hebrew discipleship training and culture puts the disciples when they were with Jesus between fifteen and eighteen years old, not balding or white-haired men. While these lenses try to tell our story—and there is some truth in them—they usually tell a version of the truth that makes us feel good when we view them. Did Jesus exist and have disciples? Yes. Do we feel much more comfortable with the idea these men God chose were learned and experienced and so their choices were thus not youthful, teenage impulses? Absolutely.

This doesn't mean everything we've learned is incorrect, nor does it mean anyone out there has "the" answer. It simply means the more I look into Christianity the more I realize there are many interpretations of the Bible and fortunately, or unfortunately, no one has the market cornered on the correct interpretation.

Throughout my years of learning, a number of scholars have made large influences on my faith. Yet as I take in their teachings, there are things that I don't necessarily agree with them on. I don't have the credentials to challenge these scholars, but as great scholars will point out, their interpretations do not necessarily challenge or dispute others' interpretations. Studies and credentials do not by themselves dictate that one person will have an advantage in discerning God's will. We all have gifts from the Lord that help us learn and discern his will. We together make up the body of Christ, and while the eye may know a lot because of the view it has, that doesn't stop the knee from feeling and knowing things through God the eye does not comprehend.

Deconstruction Begins

Let's start at the beginning. Not long ago a friend of mine had been working with a museum creating videos that talked about the beginning of the universe and how it looked from a creationist point of view. I've learned quite a bit from the discussions and the videos I've seen, but this is a new lens for me, and I'm not ready to say they are absolutely right on every detail.

This is not the beginning of a formal dialogue on the creation of the world; it's just another phase in the deconstruction pursuit of my learning and relearning. There are many answers based on scientific evidence, and many things science can help with, but there are as many mysteries in the scientific community as there are answers. In the end, science takes as much—if not more—faith than a belief in monotheism.

Some people I know cannot accept the theory of an earth only 10,000 years old. I am closer to the strict creation camp than I am the strict evolution camp, but just as I believe both theories take quite a bit of faith to believe, I also believe both camps are filled with people trying their best to understand what cannot truly be understood. There are also people on both sides who think you're either insane or destined for hell if you don't believe their way. I believe the edges of both sides are wrong. As one who walks in the footsteps of Christ, I do not believe anyone can say he or she is absolutely sure and "If you don't agree with me you're crazy or going to hell."

My evolution theory friends and I have had some good conversations over the years on the subject of creation and evolution; I've always found their insights intriguing and provoking. I share some of my opinions with them, but whether their beliefs about creation are going to keep them from heaven is God's choice; nothing I say or do will influence that decision, so why fret and worry so much about it?

The lenses with which I was taught would ask, "How can you miss a chance to bring the truth to a person so deceived? You had a chance to show the way to the lost but you didn't take it." Those seem to me to be stained glass lenses. They don't see the truth of Jesus. They are a slight reflection but not a very accurate one. Those are the lenses that say we must make converts. They are people who feel that every interaction with someone who is not saved is an opportunity to bring Christ to that person and add another notch to a belt.

Bringing Christ to people doesn't involve relationships; wisdom and whimsical, intelligent examples of Christ's love are what it takes, not building a friendship whether they believe or not. "What good is it having a great friendship with someone who ends up going to hell?" is a comment I have heard a few times in my life. But what good is it to have them say they believe but then feel as if the friendship they had was only to let the evangelist get another notch on his or her belt? The friendship goes away, and the faith doesn't usually last. People in this vein of evangelism don't tell the whole story, nor do they walk the path of the Rabbi. There's a mantra in rabbinical studies to the effect that "You want to be so close to your rabbi that the dust from his feet falls on you." The dust of my Rabbi, Christ, is definitely nowhere to be found on people who believe making converts is about the reward you get and not the relationship you develop.

In digging further in the evolution vs. creation line of thinking, for example, the six-day theory comes up quite a bit. Time is something humans created to track the days. I haven't found any references prior to the Industrial Revolution where it mattered if it was 1:15 p.m. or 2:24 a.m. Until we were paid by someone for the time we put in, minutes didn't matter. God coined the words "day" and "night" and gave us markers so we could recognize the seasons; we created the years, months, hours, minutes, and seconds to denote those spans of time. Was an hour an hour before we had watches? Yes. Did it matter if an hour was fifty-eight minutes or seventy-three minutes before we were paid by the hour? No. Yet for some people the first six days being twenty-four actual hours each is seminal, but for others, if the first six days are not allegorical, then their faith is ludicrous.

In the beginning God created the heavens and the earth, and the earth was dark. God created light and then separated the light from the dark and called the light day. This is awesome. There was light and dark at the same time and apparently the same space. There was light in the dark; they were one. There was no day or night; there were both. God then separated the light from the dark and called the light day and the dark night.

We call one day twenty-four hours. A day of work is eight hours for most employees, twelve hours for most of the medical professionals I know. A Sunday of football is about ten hours, except for Bowl Day, when it's closer to sixteen hours. We also base our days and years on the sun and the earth's rotation around it, yet the sun didn't arrive until the fourth day (Genesis 1:14-19). What is really cool is that God created the earth's plants the day before he created the sun and the moon.

Saying God created the universe in six twenty-four-hour days is just fine. But in the churches I grew up in, if you said it was any different, you were denying the entire Bible. "If it wasn't really six days, then how can you ever believe Jesus rose from the dead?"

By dictating that God had to have created the world by a method we "understand" tries to put God in a box I don't believe we should try to put him in. If God can create plants that photosynthesize before he creates the sun to make photosynthesis possible, he can do whatever else he wants. The question for me is to what end are we willing to sacrifice the relationships God brings into our lives? To set in stone that the days had to be days as we quantify them and say that anything else is a lie could potentially shut down a conversation between a believer and an unbeliever. There are a few who would respond rather acceptingly, but for the most part we wouldn't be able to develop relationships with many people because of our lens. That doesn't seem to me to be what Christ would do.

Driving Through the Rubble of Deconstruction

As we continue through the deconstruction phase, I make this point not to argue creationism. To say the Bible must be read as we in twenty-first-century America understand words is to miss the point of the Word of God entirely. The Bible was not written so we could defend God to those who don't know him. God is very clear: "If these people do not cry out the very rocks themselves will" (Luke 19:40); God's name will be proclaimed whether we do it or not. This is his creation. I have no idea whether global warming is a true crisis or just a way for scientists to get lots of money and Al Gore to stay in the spotlight without taking his clothes off or going to rehab, but I sometimes marvel at the arrogance of a humanity that thinks it can completely destroy God's creation.

When I was in my early twenties, I went over to my friend Michael's house once. He had cut down some front-yard trees, typical Michigan pines between six and eight inches across and was about to remove the stumps when I arrived. I helped him dig about a foot down all around the first stump. I axed every root I could see, even checking areas where there was nothing visible just to be sure. We then hooked up a chain between the stump and a four-by-four one-ton pickup. I got out of the way because I didn't want to get hit by the flying stump or its roots.

Michael put the truck in drive and hit the gas. When he reached the end of the chain, the truck jerked to a sudden stop. All four tires just spit up dirt; the truck would go no further. According to the commercials, trucks like this can tow incredibly large equipment and can drive up mountains. In reality, trucks like this stop dead in their tracks when they compete against the stump of a six-inch pine created by God.

When we eliminate God from our lives and think only of ourselves, it's amazing what we can come up with. Our arrogance about our "own" accomplishments in all history has been rivaled only by Lucifer in his attempted coup for the throne of heaven. Just in case you aren't sure of the final outcome, Lucifer loses.

Many people miss why God gave us the text in the first place. The purpose of the written word is to show God to us and to show us how we are to be in this life as we live in relationship with him. Unfortunately, I am as guilty of misusing the Word of God as anyone else.

I have defended and rebuked people based on my reading of the text. I have allowed pride and arrogance in my life based on the text. I have followed the seminarian's view of "If only they knew, they would understand" in talking with people about faith. But I didn't really allow the Word to create in me an obedient heart. I read to understand, to see the "truth"; I read for all the wrong reasons. I did not read to have my heart change. I did not read so through my changed heart I would obey.

We are to be obedient to what God has given us. We are not to obey only when it suits our version of God. We are to obey when it suits us and when it does not. We are to obey even if we have no idea what God is trying to say. Simply, we are to obey.

Some of the statements I've made can be taken as staunch arrogance, but that is not my intention; it's to simply and clearly state what my current walk with the Lord through obedience is producing. If I'm wrong, I pray I'll see that and change, but our world is full enough of ambiguity and poll-taking beliefs.

A while ago my oldest daughter was doing a current-events report for her class. We were looking at the news organizations on the web, and she saw a headline about the war in Iraq and was confused by the wording. It was a poll. I'm not discussing this particular war but the polls that people, especially politicians, swear by.

Later that same night a show on TV was talking about polls and how you can get a poll to say anything you want simply by changing one or two words in a question. We run our lives based on how we think other people feel about it. We choose what we do or don't do based on how other people feel about it. In the current American climate we do everything we can to make sure the majority agrees with or at least is not offended by our actions. But when you look through the Bible, the people were continually unhappy with God. In Exodus, they grumbled that they had food enough for only that day. In the establishment time of Israel, they complained they did not have a king. During Roman rule, they complained the Messiah had not come, and when he did, they killed him.

Because of the fall, it is our nature to rebel against God, to look at his wisdom and call it folly. It is our nature to want the approval of those around us and not see what the Father is doing and follow him. We cannot live as "poll" Christians. We must fight our nature and take on God's nature. And this is not just a twenty-first-century American flaw. Jesus encouraged us to

> "Be careful not to do your 'acts of righteousness' before men, to be seen by them. If you do, you will have no reward from your Father in heaven. So when you give to the needy, do not announce it with trumpets, as the hypocrites do in the synagogues and on the streets, to be honored by men. I tell you the truth, they have received their reward in full" (Matthew 6:1-2).

Men have always wanted the approval of those around them. It may be our competitive streak, it may be our desire to reconnect with our inner child, or it may the testosterone running around in our bodies, but whatever the reason, now as then we seek the approval of men.

The Bible is not here for others to learn; it is here for us. Not the "us" who are white, middle-class Americans but "us" who are the children of God. God is quite clear he will draw those he calls. Those who have the privilege and honor of knowing God also have the responsibility and duty to live in right relationship with God.

Since Adam and Eve ate the fruit, living in a right relationship with God has not been something we can grasp on our own. Knowing good and evil has given us the opportunity to choose evil as good. Most people can agree that murder, robbery, and the like are evils. But there are things that because of the Word of God we know are evil, while the majority of people in their own wisdom declare fornication, abortion, and drunkenness as moral.

One of the twenty-four-hour news channels ran an interview with a psychologist who reported that videos showing girls taking off their tops were good indicators of the idea that women were feeling positive about their bodies and that this attitude was a good thing. This is a good thing? Daughters are getting drunk and taking off their clothes, and this is good? We have taken exploitation and degradation and call it good? We have taken innocence and virtue and traded it for fifteen minutes of fame and call it self-esteem?

If we choose evil and call it good, we cannot even begin to approach God. Bonhoeffer states that even the knowledge of "other than God" in eating the fruit is the root of what separates us from God. It's not just choosing evil that separates us; it's knowing there is a choice that separates us. Simply in being able to think of "other than God" or giving ourselves or anyone else credit for God's work has forever separated us from the Creator.

Great works of art by Michelangelo, da Vinci, Picasso, or even artists who—like me—aren't very good do not mean their works of art exist apart from their creators. The statue of David cannot declare that its beauty had nothing to do with the artist who created it. But daily, if not hourly the created—humans—strut with puffed-up-chests and self-inflated-egos and state definitively that they are their own creation and that God, the artist, had nothing to do with them.

If the Bible is truly the very words of God and the laws we find ourselves restricted by do not exist for God but for us, why do we fight so hard to fit God in a box? Even if it seems for all the right, just, and pure reasons, it is never acceptable to put God in a box so things make perfect sense to us with no room left for someone to object.

When Jesus confronted people, truth always lay somewhere between the Pharisees and the pagans. Human understanding of God and human understanding of science have one very important thing in common: humans.

Lenses that Blind

This first example is just an illustration of our lenses and how we may need to rethink what we have learned and what we believe. A college professor I had said he didn't care what you believed because statistically, 95 percent of people believe what the culture around them believes. What he wanted to know was when your faith became your own, why did you believe it? What lenses did we choose to look through that let us believe Jesus was God or just a good man, that men and women are equal or not, that slavery is right or wrong, that it is okay to kill all who do not believe as we do?

In the world of Islam today, intelligent young men and women are blowing themselves up in the name of Allah. These are kids who, if born in America, would most likely be enrolling in a university and trying to figure out which fraternity or sorority to belong to. But because they are born with the lenses of modern-day jihad Islam, they are willing to kill themselves and other innocents because of a higher calling coming from someone looking through very dark lenses.

I recognize that the people who are instructing these suicide bombers believe very strongly their lenses are clear and that we infidels are looking through dark lenses. Their job, as given by Allah, is to eliminate our dark lenses.

As we look through our lenses we must remember we see through lenses that fit us as well, lenses we are comfortable with. If a person in our lives steps out of the box we see them in, it disrupts the flow of our life; we want things to stay in their proper order. But for the most part we don't see through the same lenses God does, and so quite often we try to restrict God and his work by restricting those around us and keeping them in their places.

Moses was a prince in Egypt, then he was a murderer on the run, then he was a shepherd. Through all of it he had a speech impediment. Most scholars I have encountered believe that Moses stuttered, possibly severely. No one would have picked Moses to be the voice of God because he couldn't get a straight sentence out. But God had a different set of lenses when he looked at Moses. He didn't see an obstacle; he saw faith and commitment. He didn't see an eighty-year-old, a felon on the run—he saw the leader of his people.

In making assessments and judgments about people, it's okay to keep our lenses on. I believe this is what makes us the most successful and allows us to truly enjoy what we do. I also believe that in talking with someone you care about you have to be as honest as possible, and this means letting your personal opinions and biases—your lenses—speak. In deconstructing Jesus, however, we cannot have the same attitude. We are to see Jesus as he truly is, and instead of asking him to change or not including him in our endeavors, we are to alter ourselves so we reflect him regardless of where we personally want to be. There is tremendous wisdom in a friend telling you you may want to further develop certain skills; no question about that. But that is very different from saying, "Here the Bible just seems to be a little too restrictive for me" or "I don't think God would ever really do that, so I don't believe that part of the Bible."

I'm going to jump around a bit and not just follow a biblical time line in my discussion of deconstructing the text. When I was in college, I was a counselor at a Christian camp during one particular week for campers with disabilities ranging from slight Down syndrome to severe mental and physical handicaps; they were to learn about Jesus and have a great time. This particular year we had a chaplain everyone loved. He was a physically strong man—very rugged looking and tough when it came to work, but he had the gentlest spirit of anyone I'd ever met up to then. He was very intriguing to me, and I liked quite a lot of what he was teaching that week.

I don't remember the exact words that put up my "but what about . . ." antennae, but he said something about God never hurting anyone. After the main session I had a chance to ask him how he was able to say that in light of the Old Testament writings where God required that every conquered man, woman, and child must die or the Israelites would be punished, or David's request in the Psalms that God would "dash the babies' heads on the rocks" (Psalm 137:9). He looked at me and with every conviction of truth in his heart said that I had given great examples, and other stories like it in the Old Testament were the reason he thought the Old Testament was a good book to read but actually held no authority whatsoever. It was not God as he knew God, so it must not really be God but a way for writers of that time to scare people into obeying.

This chaplain could not reconcile a God who demanded that children must die with the God he'd come to know. So instead of trying to see past his own horror to the truth of Scripture, he simply dismissed the passage and altered who God was to fit what he felt comfortable with.

He is not alone in what he did. Paul's requirements for church leaders are quite strict, but how many church leaders do we know who don't fit Paul's criteria for a leader? And still we allow them into leadership. Despite how they live, how their families live, what they reflect to those around them, we say, "Randy is a good man, so it's okay."

According to Paul it's not okay. How many times do you hear gossip in church and people let it go because "she's old" or some other excuse. A former president of a seminary had to step down from his position there and in the denomination he served because he married his daughter and her lesbian lover. The part that makes me shake my head is that not only was it a tough battle to have him removed, he also had many, many supporters stating that what he did had been good.

How we treat and live with people who are involved in homosexuality is something I think needs to be and should be discussed, but I believe absolutely that homosexuality is not what God planned and as such should not be flaunted in God's face. Nonetheless, some people would be very angry at me for stating this opinion and use biblical interpretations to show me how wrong I was and that my thoughts and actions were truly evil.

We justify what we are comfortable with. We justify what we don't want to be mean about. We justify actions because we don't know what else to do. I believe having a daughter who is a lesbian would bring a whole new dynamic to your faith walk, but instead of changing who we are to fit God, we change God to fit who we are. We change God to fit the new knowledge we have acquired, to make our feelings okay. We change God to better fit in with society so society's members will not be so reluctant to come into the fold. In a world of intolerance and injustice we decide it would be better to change God so he was more appealing and tolerant than to ask that we, the creation, change and deny our innate feelings.

Obedience can be harmful if not viewed with the proper lenses. One Christmas, when I was helping my brother with his work Christmas party, I heard a conversation during which someone said, "I'm not that religion; I'm Catholic." The other religion they were talking about was Protestantism. I'd heard this sentiment quite a bit in my life, having grown up Protestant in a predominantly Catholic area. It's an issue most people don't think about because their lenses don't differentiate the pain that comes with it, but it does affect the unity God calls us to and our relationship with Christ and others who are God's children. I will state this as emphatically as I can: Catholicism is not a different religion. It is a different denomination. Catholics have different practices and different theories, but they are not non-Christians.

Divisions such as this may not seem to hurt the body of Christ. I'm around Protestants who don't really know any practicing Catholics. It's not that they have a strong disagreement with anyone in particular; they just live in a predominantly Protestant area. But I believe this is a tool Satan uses to keep the body of Christ in turmoil. If the eyes don't realize or acknowledge that the ears exist, the body suffers. If the feet try to do everything because they don't want to associate with the hands, the body will not be able to get much accomplished. Divisions between Catholicism and Protestantism have led to divisions between Baptists and Lutherans, between members of the Assembly of God and those of the Church of Christ; between Reformed and Christian Reformed. Believe it or not, in the Reformed tradition there are Reformed, Christian Reformed, Baptist Reformed, Protestant Reformed, Dutch Reformed, Netherlands Reformed, Congregationalist Reformed, Presbyterian Reformed, Confederation of Reformed Evangelicals, Evangelical Reformed, Free Reformed Church, Heritage Netherlands Reformed, Orthodox Christian Reformed, Reformed Episcopal Church, Reformed Presbyterian in the United States, Sovereign Grace Ministries, United Reformed Church in North America, and United Church of Christ.

These are just the names of denominations I know by working around the Reformed Church in America and with a ministry loosely associated with it; there may be more I'm not aware of. The reformed branches of the Protestant wing of Christianity are not that big, and look how divisive they have become. It can start with well-intentioned theses, ninety-five, for instance, but it usually ends up with questions about which version of the hymnal is the correct one, whether children should be allowed to receive communion, and whether women should be allowed to speak in church. This never ending spiral leads us away from instead of toward Christ. It shows the world we can't get along with people who basically agree with us, so how will we ever get along with someone who is gay, divorced, or an evolutionist? We push God's children away for the sake of being like Christ, but Jesus continually called people toward him and did not let those around him keep outsiders away. For the sake of the "purity" of the master we have set our acceptance standards so high that Jesus himself could not hurdle them.

Lenses that Alienate

I have some problems with almost every Christian denomination, and Catholicism is no exception. But Catholics do not have a different faith. As I think about it, that is the crux of the matter for me with the "this or nothing" faiths: Those that demand you see God and the Gospels in light of their understanding. Those that demand you see faith as they do or it is not genuine. Those that demand you become just like them or you'll go to hell. Those that demand that no matter what body part you have, you should behave and look just like their part.

Catholics have done a tremendous job in an area that Protestantism seems to have failed miserably in: community. Catholicism is very community-oriented at its roots, while Protestantism is "Jesus and me" oriented.

In the Bible Paul talks about our being the body of Christ. In our arrogance and our humanistic tendencies, we assume that Paul is "correctly" talking about us as individuals. But what English does not do with the word "you" is let us know if it is singular or plural. Does Paul mean you or you all?

Fortunately, Greek differentiates between the singular and the plural second-person pronoun, and in the cases where the Bible is talking about "You are the body of Christ" (1 Corinthians 12:27), "you" is plural. You, Mike Shmoe, are not the body of Christ or the temple of Christ all by yourself. You and other believers in your sphere of influence are the body of Christ. You and all the Christians who've come before, are now in the world with you, and are to come make up the temple of God.

In the Protestantism I grew up around, we are Americans first and Christians second. We are "pull yourself up by your own bootstraps" and "God helps those who help themselves" God-fearing Americans. We are individuals who happen to get together to worship God. We say, "I don't want you to butt into my spiritual life, and I definitely don't want to be in yours. Unless, of course, your expression of faith begins to wander too far from what I think is right; then I'll be happy to let you know how to get back on track."

When I look within the Catholic churches around me and focus on the people, I have mostly found communities that truly care about each other and are deeply involved in each other's lives. For every Catholic church example I give, someone will be able to show me one that does not model this; nothing is absolute when people are involved. But for the most part Catholics are rooted in each other. They know each other. It is engrained in their doctrine, and they take that very seriously.

Once you get above a certain-sized group, true community is not possible. I'm not talking about churches with a few dozen people or even a few hundred people but churches with a weekly attendance of 10,000 people. There is no way anyone can have a close community involving all the people: it's just too big. This is not to argue that there is no place for megachurches; it is simply to comment on the ability of true community to exist in them. I've been in 125-member Protestant congregations whose people aren't in community with one another. If they even notice each other on Sunday morning it's a surprise, a pleasant surprise, but a surprise nonetheless.

Both major types of Christianity I have talked about have good points and bad points. The overall point I want to make is that both need each other; both should desire the same thing, a relationship with the Creator of all things.

If you are not involved in the lives of the people around you, you are in danger of making faith simply lip service or fire insurance. We exchange pleasantries and social, superficial conversations and never bother to really get involved. If churchgoers really look at their lives and look at what they show as important, they may see a reflection of arrogance and self-centeredness that rivals dictators and divas throughout time. We are not called to live lives of just striving for what we want; we are called to live the lives God calls us to live regardless of what that looks like.

When I first moved to Holland, Michigan, I was a young Christian looking for a church. I met a couple of people through the holiest of all games, *Monday Night Football.* I asked them about church, and they told me about theirs. I asked one of them why he had chosen his church, and he told me that it was close to his house. When I pressed a little further, he said he didn't really like church, but if he didn't go to a church in this community he would go out of business. Going to church for him was good business. The sad part of this is my friend is not the only one. Church for many people is a social—or business-networking system that has good people involved in it. It just makes sense to get your customers from a place that requires honesty and integrity.

Lenses that Shine

The aforementioned Jordyn has greatly influenced me and my faith. When it comes to me and things I understand, I feel I'm pretty daring and carefree. When it comes to going to a different country where Christians and Americans are really hated, I tend to completely avoid any discussion of heading there no matter what God may be saying. If God is saying "Go to a place where you have a chance of dying because of what you believe or how you look," I tell God that he's made a mistake but I forgive him. As of this writing God has not asked that of me yet, so while I know my nature would be to say no, I haven't had to actually say it.

Jordyn was home over Christmas, and I talked with her a little about what she is and will be doing. She said she truly misses home and her family; she would like nothing better than to just come home and be safe with people she loves. But she has also been feeling a call to missions and getting involved in them one hundred percent. Because of the call and her personal feelings, I figured she would be coming home and going to work at a soup kitchen, practicing "mission," and being safe. Not Jordyn. She is planning on going to mission school in Mozambique during the summer. Mozambique? I'm not sure where in Africa that is, but I'm sure there are high risks in going, especially for a beautiful American girl. She acknowledged some of the warnings she'd heard, but God was calling, and she did not want to miss out on his blessings and adventure. Once again I am in awe and humbled by this tremendous woman of God. I am a very large, thick male, and I am nervous. Here is a beautiful, athletic woman walking into the gates of hell. But she knows that as she goes, she is walking with God, and Jesus promised her that when God goes with her, "even the gates of hell will not prevail against her" (Matthew 16:18).

My lenses say that if my life will be in danger, I avoid that trip. Bill Cosby, a marvelous philosopher and comedian, once said, "If you eat shrimp and later your face blows up, you don't eat that shrimp again." I guess the lenses I've grown up with follow that logic very strongly. If they give you a warning to not ever go out alone, I assume it's best to avoid that place altogether.

Over the last decade or so we have all seen enough images of different countries' citizens chanting hatred toward Americans. We realize that just being white and speaking a Yankee version of English is enough to get us killed in certain areas. But where does obedience lie when looking through those lenses? At this particular point in my life I'm not able to take those lenses off and look at God fully, but I pray every day that God will continue to give me the strength and the faith to do so. With God and friends such as Jordyn I believe one day I'll remove those lenses and see God more clearly.

Lenses of Culture

I love Canadians. I have had a wonderful affinity for them for quite a while. In seminary I met Rob, a Canadian. Even though he said he was a Christian, he used one particular word a lot that in my family was considered profanity. At first I wasn't sure how to approach this topic, but he noticed my shock. He laughed and said he'd forgotten I didn't know that in Canada "s#!t" was not considered profane. It was the same as saying "crap" or "darn" or any of the other "polite" words we have here in America. As I've met more Canadians, I've come to realize that they do not all hold this belief and that Rob was most likely speaking from his cultural circle. But I did admire the freedom he felt.

The lenses I viewed words through came mostly from my parents. My mom always wanted us to be articulate but polite. Words such as this were definitely off our linguistic map. In fact, if she reads this, she'll be embarrassed that I came close to actually printing the word in this book.

This is not to defame or defend certain words but to say there are some things we take for granted and give biblical weight to even though the Bible isn't as specific as we would sometimes like. This is a call to evaluate our biblical lenses so we aren't denying someone a relationship with the living God over something as small as a word.

I try to give people the benefit of the doubt; people have good intentions when they gain understanding. Either through personal study or divine revelation they have discovered something they feel is right. They've had the almighty "ah-ha" moment. Once they become convinced they're right, they are sure that this is not the answer just for them but "the" answer. Subsequently, everyone who professes in a similar fashion should profess this "ah-ha" as well. When they domino effect this difference, it inevitably leads to the questioning of or the disbelief in the death and resurrection of Jesus. It could not be six literal twenty-four-hour days, so Christ must not have really risen from the tomb, right?

If the ark didn't really exist, then Jesus must not have either, huh? God is greater than that. God is greater than our small differences. God is greater than human proof. God is greater than human physics. When it comes to God and science, God *is* science. But science is our small, very thick, and dingy lens we use to try to understand what God has created.

Just as we are all parts of one body in function and in gifting, we are also part of one body in understanding. There are foods that (in my opinion) smell wretched but taste pretty good. Just because my nose says it is foul does not mean my tongue agrees. Just because my eyes say a snake's skin must be wet, bumpy, and rough doesn't mean my hands feel anything but a smooth, dry surface. Can the foot tell the hand it does not need it to feed the body? No . . . wait. For people born without arms or who have been in an accident and no longer have arms, yes. Oops. Can the hands tell the feet they do not need them to walk? Well, some people with no legs have found amazing ways of getting around by using their hands and arms. Just because one part of the body has an understanding of the way things work does not mean the whole body is subject to that same understanding.

The head adjusts the body to fit the circumstances and advantages or disadvantages it encounters. Since Christ is the head and we are not, we can offer our ideas and even present apologetics as to why it should be this way. But in the end, it is only the head that truly knows the difference. The body adjusts and assumes what the head tells it. While hands may one day need to be feet, they will never be the head.

Catholicism and Catholic friends have been a huge influence in my life on developing community, insula. Catholics are very good at community. The "Jesus and me" stance of Protestantism missed the mark on community and I think we need to grab hold of what Catholics have discovered.

The Protestant work ethic of picking yourself up by your bootstraps is not only not a biblical principle, it actually goes against physics as well. If you are stuck in the mud and try to pull yourself out by your bootstraps, the force needed to get your feet out actually pushes you deeper into the mud, and you get hopelessly stuck.

It doesn't work on a farm, and it doesn't work in the kingdom of God. But at least for me and others brought up in the same cultural circumstances, those are the lenses we see through.

Lenses that Transform

As I continue with our lenses, I'll mention one I am growing in and learning about more every day, grace. At least in this area the Reformed Church and other denominations like it have done a marvelous job of bringing grace and the love of God out over the oppressive, judgmental God who was shown to the world during times the Spanish Inquisition. (Monty Python fans, repeat with me, "*Nobody* expects the Spanish Inquisition.") But we have let the pendulum of grace swing so far that it has neutered Jesus. We can see Jesus only as a calm, caring, forgiving man. We are afraid, from the sins of the past in events like the Spanish Inquisition, that if we show anything but acceptance and grace we will drive people from, not toward, Christ. We have taken offensive language, thoughts, and actions out of our faith and replaced them with a big, fluffy bunny that would never hurt a flea. That is not what the text calls us to. The text has places for grace and love, but it also has a place for the tougher side of God's love. Because writing doesn't allow inflection, the calm, caring words should be said with a hint of a Ted Knight or a Holiday Inn lounge-singer voice. Psalm 111:10a states, "The fear of the LORD is the beginning of wisdom"; we have taken the word "fear" and have substituted the word "respect" to not offend anyone.

For twenty-plus years I ran sound for a music ministry duo, leading worship weekends, conferences, and such. Many times I would hear a speaker talk about fearing the Lord as really respecting the Lord and giving him what is due just as you would respect a teacher or community leader or the president. But that is not what the words of God say. Over thirty times throughout the Bible we are told to "fear God." We are also told,

> If you are not careful to observe all the words of this law which are written in this book, to fear this honored and awesome name, the LORD your God, then the LORD will bring extraordinary plagues on you and your descendants, even severe and lasting plagues, and miserable and chronic sicknesses. (Deuteronomy 28:58-59)

The lenses I was taught with said that God is loving and full of grace. He would never do anything to let you go or leave you. Satan wanted to hurt you. Satan wanted you to be afraid of him, and God was not like Satan at all. I agree that God is not like Satan, but I believe our human eyes got it completely wrong. Satan wants to be our buddy, our friend. He wants to be the one who gives us what we "really" want and not the things that are truly good for us. Satan wants us to do it ourselves; we don't need a "God" to fight through the hypocrisy of the world and through the muck and mire that exists; we alone can conquer the world.

God says, 'You are my child, and I love you, but I cannot let your sins go.' God says, 'I will give you everything your heart desires, but you must follow my words.' God says, "Take up my yoke, for my burden is light." God also says, "Do not lay a hand on the boy. Do not do anything to him. Now I know that you fear God, because you have not withheld from me your son, your only son" (Genesis 22:12).

God stopped Abraham from killing Isaac not because he had been a good servant, not because he was faithful in leaving his land, not because he was God's favorite. The angel said, "Now I know that you fear God, because you have not withheld from me your son, your only son." Abraham was so fearful of God's wrath that he was willing to kill Isaac to avoid it.

In Christianity in America today, to publicly proclaim those words would be blasphemy. We don't want an angry God who requires us to live his way; we want a forgiving God who sees us and loves us in spite of the wrong things we do and will gladly accept us into paradise because we said the name "Jesus" as we talked about God.

Let's look at Ananias and Sapphira as an example. This is a very good lesson about lying to the Lord; if you read the passage closely you'll see that's all they did. As far as we know they were faithful people, "regulars," because Peter knew who they were, and they had been blessed by God, in property at least. They sold some, not all, of their property and kept some, not all, of the proceeds. They knew the apostles expected them to give all the money from the sale of the property to the church. They may have made that arrangement previously, or it may have been a general understanding. "There were no needy persons among them. For from time to time those who owned lands or houses sold them, brought the money from the sales and put it at the apostles' feet, and it was distributed to anyone as he had need"(Acts 4:34-35).

Ananias and Sapphira did what they thought was okay. Maybe they were greedy; maybe they had a problem with Thaddaeus (he never caused any noteworthy disagreements among Jesus and the disciples, but it's a thought); maybe they just wanted a longer vacation. For whatever reason they withheld some of the money. There's conjecture about why they lied. Ananias could have been prideful or scared; Peter had cut off an ear of one of the guards who came for Jesus, and James and John were the sons of thunder, not the sons of lilies. The disciples had a reputation of being godly but also somewhat brash and impulsive, not people you'd want to confess to.

When Ananias brings the money from the sale, at least as those around knew, Peter doesn't give him an out or press him for the truth and pass judgment. He asks,

> Ananias, how is it that Satan has so filled your heart that you
> have lied to the Holy Spirit and have kept for yourself some
> of the money you received for the land? Didn't it belong

> to you before it was sold? And after it was sold, wasn't the
> money at your disposal? What made you think of doing such
> a thing? You have not lied to men but to God. (Acts 5:3-4)

With that Ananias fell dead. No grace. No love. No "Oh that's alright; you have learned a valuable lesson, my young Jedi. Next time do not withhold from the Lord." He was just dead.

Three hours later Sapphira comes in. She hasn't seen Ananias, doesn't realize he's dead from lying. Ananias had told her and had received her blessing on the scam; maybe she wanted a new pair of shoes. When confronted, she backed her husband. How many times have we seen people defending their spouses when the latter mess up? We almost always see that as admirable, and if not, we definitely understand why they did it. Not God. Once again, Peter doesn't give grace or love. He asks, "'How could you agree to test the Spirit of the Lord? Look! The feet of the men who buried your husband are at the door, and they will carry you out also.' At that moment she fell down at his feet and died" (Acts 5:9-10).

This is a God to be afraid of. This is a God not to mess with because he's greater and more powerful than anything we have seen. He doesn't want our respect or our kowtowing. He wants our fear and our love. It is a dichotomy we can't often reconcile with our lives and with our own sense of morality. This is not the Sunday school God I learned about or the God of the 1980s television evangelists; this is a God we prefer to avoid.

God is about calling us to live in community with him. But to truly live in community with God, we cannot expect him to come down to our level; we must rise to his. God cannot come down to our tolerant, accepting ways. We must clean up our act and begin to live as Christ did. We must strive to "be perfect as your heavenly father is perfect" (Matthew 5:48).

But this is also not the God of my grandparents' generation. This is not a God that is without grace and forgiveness. This is not a God waiting for you to mess up so he can squish you like a little bug. This is a God our human understanding cannot quite grasp, and so we lie, we take a small part of God and proclaim that image to be the complete God.

As part of our deconstruction we must scrape off and throw away our nifty bumper stickers such as "Christians aren't perfect—just forgiven." That's not what the Bible says or how we should present ourselves to the world. That's not how we should live, but we live every day with phrases like that. We need to change our thoughts of what God calls us to so we reflect him and not the pleasant world around us.

We live in a society so repulsed by the thought of God that a lawsuit is threatened when a student tries to quote from Scripture at a graduation ceremony. Our society is so reviled by God that when a group of committed, young people gather and pray that those offended by Proposition 8 come to know God in a personal way and see his desire for their lives, they receive harsh and most intolerant criticism because of what they believe.

This is not a country of Christian values; this is a country of modified values based on legal precedent and conventional wisdom but mostly on the wisdom of those who have received credentials from our institutions and those with the ability and/or financing to bring their fights to court when they don't get their own way.

We are not living in a culture that values the Word of God. We live in a post-Christian society bent on dominance. We live in a culture in which we are responsible for all the good around us and are working on ways to eliminate all the consequences of the lives we lead.

Our culture has crept through the cracks and has influenced how we see and interpret Christ and the text. We need to take a step back, deconstruct that which we believe, hold it up to the light of Scripture, and see where we have been looking with lenses that are too shaded for us to truly see God. We need to deconstruct what we know, what we think we know, and what we are planning on passing on. We need to look with fresh lenses and put aside the shades of the culture around us.

CHAPTER 4

A Lack of Faith in the Evidence of Experience

Who are you who is so wise in the ways of science?
—Sir Bedivere

I had a different beginning for this chapter, but as I went over it I realized it needed more. Lack of faith is something every believer struggles with from time to time. It may not be a life crisis; it may not last more than a minute or two. We all have doubts about faith and about God's work in our lives. But it seems in American Christianity today we have taken those doubts and transformed them into a healthy belief system, one that doesn't intrude on our worldly obligations.

As believers in the Bible we are allowed moments of doubt. The text is riddled with the stories of people who were faithful followers of God but had moments of doubt. We have taken that moment of doubt and turned it into a healthy skepticism so that we are not too fanatical but not too depraved.

Faith is something we have. Whether it is faith in God, our family, a sports team, or science, we all have a belief in something greater than our individual selves. To quote Steve Martin, "I guess I wouldn't believe in anything if it wasn't for my lucky astrology mood watch."

There are facts, things we assume are facts, and things we have no factual evidence for but until evidence to the contrary comes to light we accept as fact. To get to the root of faith and how it relates to us and in turn how we relate to God, I will throw out these three posits on fact.

Things that are fact: The earth is round. Whales are mammals.

Things we assume are fact: Dinosaurs no longer live on earth. Flying is safer than driving.

Things there is no factual evidence of but we believe anyway: Evolution. You must wait thirty minutes after eating before swimming.

Matter of Fact

"Fact" as defined by Merriam-Webster is "something that has actual existence . . . an actual occurrence . . . a piece of information presented as having objective reality."

Taking the first definition into account, there are things that people presume are facts that absolutely are not facts. There is not actual existence of many things we have labeled fact. A quick example of this is our monetary system. We used to base our monetary value on gold, hence the saying "he who has all the gold makes all the rules." Throughout the twentieth century the powers that be fluctuated between the gold standard system and the fiat system. In 1973 the federal government went back to the fiat system, and the worth of our dollar has been based in cyberspace ever since.

We say one dollar is worth just that, but with nothing concrete to base our value on, all we have is the assurance that people will believe what they have been told to keep the value of our dollar where it is. If enough people disagree with the powers that be, the fact of the dollar becomes a moot point and shifts to whatever prevailing winds are proclaiming.

Most of the things we call facts are not necessarily absolute. They have been proven true in our experience, and so we claim them to be facts. We fall back on Pontius Pilate's question, "What is truth?" in stating that facts are not necessarily true for everyone.

One online video, "Peter Schiff gets it right on the economy," is a series of news talk shows with different economic "experts" telling us what the economy is going to do. There are times where the two experts are stating the exact opposite. In one instance, from November 2007, two men are talking about the stock market; one says with absolute confidence that by November 2008 the Dow is going to be over 16,000. Peter Schiff, the other expert, disagrees completely and says the Dow will fall to almost 8,000. As the market dropped I wondered how those experts who predicted that our economy would do great couldn't have been more wrong. But many people believed the positive-economy people and denied the evidence in front of them. How can someone who is an expert get it so wrong?

Al Gore made a movie about global warming and proclaimed his message to all who would listen. His movie showed how "man-made" global warming was destroying the earth. He won an Oscar and the Nobel Peace Prize for this movie and got people around the world to notice the wretched things man is doing to the earth. Recently, over 650 noted scientists have voiced opposition to the theory of man-made global warming. So is the Nobel Peace Prize, Oscar-winning politician right, or are the scientists? Both sides proclaim they have the facts and the truth on their sides, but they both can't be right. You cannot have the same facts and come to two oppositely true conclusions.

Facts don't appear to be factual at all; they seem more a platform of evidence that we interpret, and those interpretations then become our facts.

John F. Kennedy was shot and killed in November 1963. According to the Warren Commission, Lee Harvey Oswald was a lone assassin, not a member of a conspiracy, who had good aim and quick reflexes. For hard-core conspiracy theorists and thousands if not tens of thousands of people, the facts are such that it could not have been one lone gunman. If you Google "Kennedy conspiracy," you'll come across more than 308,000 sites on this subject. The evidence doesn't conclusively support a single shooter or a vast conspiracy, but the government, including the court system, maintains that the facts point to a lone gunman, and the conspiracy theorists will never believe it was anything but a massive cover-up.

CSI and the other such shows are all about evidence and facts. I love these shows; they are amazing mysteries that engage and entertain. The creators, writers, actors, and everyone else involved should be very proud. But at the same time, as O.J. Simpson's trial in the 1990s proved that evidence can be interpreted in a variety of ways. Simply because we have evidence does not mean we have facts. Because the glove did not fit, a man got away with murdering his ex-wife and an innocent bystander because he had an amazing legal team able to show the evidence was not the facts of the case.

More Hats

We throw the word "fact" around as if it were an absolute. In researching this thought process I came across quite a few websites that challenge the fact that the earth revolves around the sun. They are using the Bible to show the earth is stationary, at the center of the universe, and the rest of the universe—the sun, the planets and all the stars in the heavens—revolve around us.

These are not first—or second-century books; these are modern websites using modern data to support this "fact." This diatribe is not meant to discuss the possibility that the earth is stationary but just to show that people can formulate "facts" that use the same evidence to support their understanding and belief regardless of other theories.

Sometimes those "facts" of science don't even involve science. One of my professors in graduate school stated that global warming was a fact and as evidence of that he stated that people were wearing hats much more in Australia. Other readings and studies he had come across brought him to that determination, but the evidence that he used to try to convince us was "more hats."

This seems to be the same type of evidence we use in our lives. We see the actions, the facts around us, and we grasp an understanding based on the information we see. We then formulate a hypothesis and do some internal testing. The testing is not to prove our hypothesis and thus transform it into a theory but to see if anything contradictory is more convincing. If we cannot find anything more persuasive, then our hypothesis becomes theory and, for us, fact.

I'm not taking sides on these issues because I cannot fully understand all their complexities and nuances. They are simply my basis for the fact that facts aren't facts at all but the results of interpretations of information.

In the 1980 movie *The Gods Must Be Crazy*, a tribal man finds a soda bottle; it's the first time he has ever seen such a product of modern technology. When he brings it to his village, many bad things happen, so it is determined that the bottle must be evil and must be returned to the God who gave it to them.

The people of this tribe thought that things had been going fairly well until the gods gave them this thing, and then things started going badly. The fact: since this thing arrived we have had bad luck, so we must give it back. The modern world would consider their thoughts as superstitious, but these people believed it to be fact. Both parties have the same evidence, but because of circumstance and experience they interpret it differently.

Similar real-life events have happened. In 1692, in Salem, Massachusetts, the overactive imaginations of grown adults and the manipulating control of four young girls sent nineteen men and women to their deaths and hundreds more to jail because of the "fact" they were witches. We know they were not witches, but to those people it was fact; they murdered innocent people because of this.

In the story of the Tower of Babel the people are building a tower to reach the heavens. God states that if they are able to accomplish this, there is nothing they will not be able to do. Most biblical historians estimate the tower of Babel was between three hundred and five hundred feet tall when God confused their languages and the building project was disbanded.

Today, five-hundred foot buildings are by no means unimaginable. We have surpassed what the people of Babel did, and now we're talking about colonizing the moon. We have reached the height of humanity; there seems almost nothing we cannot accomplish. But even in the midst of our modern, technological, advanced age there are still things we cannot fully grasp: an unexpected healing, a lost child found alive, Carrot Top selling out in Las Vegas. Some say these are coincidences, some say karma, some say miracles.

Rotting from Within

My discussion is not about people who do not see the miracles of God because they do not believe in a higher power. I am looking at something much more offensive and much more insidious. Christians are daily overlooking miracles of God and calling them fate, coincidence, or "knock on wood" luck. We have bought into the modern American view of science and our own self-inflated cause-and-effect theory. No longer do we see unexplained things as coming from God's hand; we now call them chance, or preparation meeting perseverance, or one of any of the numerous quips motivational speakers throw out to show you are worth something and you can do it. We have forgotten the true premise of our lives: that on our own we are not able to do anything. No matter how many nuclear bombs we set off, the sun will still rise tomorrow. No matter how many cars we drive, the mountains will still stand. No matter how many coffee shops we build, the miracle of birth will not diminish one bit.

For some reason we have eliminated God's hand in this world to accommodate a human-labeled set of laws under which we believe all things must operate. The human laws I speak of were created by God; it's just that we have identified them and in so doing have claimed them as our own.

I have come across a sect of Christians I did not know existed until recently. They are Christians who believe the first eleven chapters of Genesis are myth. By myth I don't mean they are uncertain that the earth was created in six twenty-four-hour days or a longer period, or even that Adam and Eve were real or representational. I mean they believe the creation and Adam and Eve are as real as Hogwarts and Harry Potter. These are people who say that they believe in Jesus Christ as the Son of God and that they have a savior who has redeemed their souls and paid the price for their sins so that they may experience eternity with God. They call the work of God not literal or illustrative but actual myth, a fake, a brilliant work of fiction.

If you cannot bring yourself to believe in a higher power, I can understand how you would be unable to believe there is an intelligent designer who has constructed the world around you. What I don't grasp in any way is how they think God "[l]oved the World so much that he gave his only son, that whoever believes in him would not perish but would have eternal life" (John 3:16) and yet do not believe this same God, this same Lord of all, could create the world. This is probably the greatest example of a lack of faith in the evidence of fact I have found. But daily we overlook things that are in the same vein as this situation and call it "healthy skepticism."

Once, while she was in a tremendous hurry, my bride entered a very busy intersection. When she pulled up, there was no cross traffic coming, and this almost never happened. It usually takes only three to five minutes when you normally arrive at this intersection to pull out safely, but as anyone knows when you are late and in a hurry, three to five minutes is longer than a bad zombie movie.

When she arrived at her destination she mentioned the intersection to some coworkers. She said, without fully realizing it, "God blessed me on that one." A fellow coworker we know to be a believer in Christ asked, "What makes you think that God cares about whether you are on time or not?" He was truly confused and somewhat disgusted with someone crediting the timing of traffic to God. And yet this is a believer. This is someone who supposedly believes God is concerned enough about us all to know the numbers of hairs on our heads and to send his Son to die in our place, concerned enough to take the time, energy, and effort to reach out to each of us in the individual way we need and reaches us for Christ. But this person cannot see how God is blessing us and watching out for us in the small, simple things.

We have continued the Greek tradition of viewing the human being as the ultimate in the existence of life. We have images of the perfect, six-pack-abs-people standing in intriguing poses; we have testimonies of the brilliance of the minds of people such as Einstein, Darwin, or Hawking; we strut gorgeous men and women up and down ramps showing how beautiful we have become. We have been able to achieve everything we have ever wanted. We have shows on how rich people live—"Don't you wish you could live like this too?" Human beings and their accomplishments have become the height of our ambitions. We no longer try to imitate the Creator of the world; we are too busy trying to become the next rich superstar.

Those we place on the pedestal of success and achievement are typically the loneliest and most troubled. People with a tremendous amount of fame and money seem to be the most-frequent visitors at rehab clinics, or perhaps they have realized the destruction that drugs can cause and have turned over a new leaf and see a better way for us all to live.

Where Have They Gone?

My daughter once asked me why events like Shadrach, Meshach, and Abednego in the furnace didn't happen anymore. I realized things like that didn't seem to happen anymore in America. I have heard of stories from Third World countries that would have impressed those three brothers, but in America we have lost so much of our faith to science and natural selection that God chooses not to work miracles here.

When Jesus healed people he almost always said, "[Y]our faith has made you well." Your faith, not his faith; your faith, not the faith of the Father for his purposes; your faith, not the collective cry of a united nation but the faith of the person who had belief and chutzpah enough to ask Jesus for something impossible.

We—American Christians—have given up our faith for a happier, safer way of life. We do not have a king forcing us to bow and worship him instead of God, but we do have a society that has moved from living as our Creator intended to living as the Constitution allows. We have a society in which a comedian can state boldly that you're stupid if you don't believe in evolution, and the audience cheers and laughs.

Our society as a whole, including a vast majority of Christians, has written creation off as a myth. We have taken the words of God and have called them myth. We have taken the acts of God and called them mystic explanations we now can see through rational eyes. We have lost our faith. Mark 6 tells us that Jesus, God incarnate himself, could do no miracles in his own hometown because of that people's lack of faith. If Jesus could not do miracles in a place because of the lack of faith there, what makes us think we will be able to do any better?

Faith is God-given, but unless we take it up and carry it as our own, it does nothing. We are just as the residents of Jesus' hometown: we have lost our faith. Not only as a country or as a community but unbelievably as followers of the living God we have chosen the explanation of those around us and have abandoned God. Every day God does amazing miracles in our midst, yet we refuse to acknowledge him or give him the glory.

My hero in faith, Jordyn, went to Africa for a summer of mission learning after her freshman year in college. Everything was going fine, and she was really experiencing God's love and grace. A week before she was to come home she began to show symptoms of malaria. A group of us immediately began praying and calling others to pray for her. We forwarded emails from her family to our friends to keep them up to date with her condition. It appeared that Jordyn was getting better and would be able to make her flight back to the States. At the end of that email the author wrote "Yea, God!" One of my family members replied, "Yea, God?" This family member just could not understand why we would attribute this to God. Jordyn had been given medicine and was taking precautions to make sure she would recover. This wasn't God; this was pure science.

Yet I say, "Yea, God!" Was it the pills she began taking after the symptoms arrived? Sure. Was it the cold cloths and the four days of rest under a table on a cool, cement floor? Sure. I will concede all that but only with the understanding that God is the Creator of everything.

How many times have we seen or heard of medicine not working? How many times have medical professionals and scientists been wrong? How many times can we not explain why it didn't work? God is no less responsible for Jordyn's healing because she took a pill; God is responsible for all the blessings in our lives.

By giving glory and credit to ourselves and our achievements we have changed the relationship with our Creator. We have twisted around our praises to God and have instead blamed God. We now call the blessings "luck" or "science" and blame God for the misfortunes and the tragedies in our lives. But God does not bring calamity on us—sin does. God does not bring death and disease into our lives—sin does. God does not take little children and kill them—sin does. Yet when this world rears its ugly head we look to the heavens and ask, "Why did God do this?" or "Why did God let this happen?" We refuse to see the sin that envelops us and the sin in our daily lives that destroys a little bit of us each minute; we put it all on God's shoulders instead.

Others, though, do not put the calamity on God, sighting that God will not curse you if you don't pray (or have faith); they're more arrogant than those who don't see blessings from God. They argue with you if you state you needed to pray or lean on God to get his blessing. They assume that just because they sometimes live their lives in faith or when they were ten they said a prayer that God would bless them continually. They don't see any reason for daily interaction with God, and they laugh at anyone who tries to make that connection. Their arrogance grows because when they talk they give God credit continually and talk as if they are deeply reliant on God, but when you watch their actions, they are far from God and don't reach to him at all. They too have given in to the world's perspective and tried not to look hard at the things of God because they wish to seem wise.

Every Chance We Get

In Joshua, the Israelites are deceived by a kingdom not because God cursed them but because they did not inquire of the Lord in the matter, and it cost the Israelites greatly. They are the chosen people of God. God himself refers to Israel as his firstborn. If God withholds his blessings even from the Israelites for using their wisdom, what arrogance must it take to assume we can do the same with better results?

It seems we turn from God every chance we get and still expect God to remain faithful to us and bless us and do so in the ways we want. We mock him, defy him, alter his Word to fit our definitions of tolerance and wisdom in the name of enlightenment and still expect him to deliver what we want.

Here's a statement about Satan that is vital and relevant to Christians in today's world: "The best lie Satan ever told was getting people to believe that he doesn't exist."

In not acknowledging Satan/our sins, we can deny that he/they exist at all. In denying they exist, there is no reason for repentance. In denying there is sin, we negate any standards that point to a better way, standards that show the way we are proceeding is wrong. If we deny sin, we can deny God. If we deny God, we have only ourselves. In having only ourselves, we have the ultimate creator: us.

My uncle, a certified genius, has a rather high I.Q. He's spent his life in a philosophical endeavor that most would find tedious and much too complex. He doesn't believe in a God; in fact, his thought process has taken him down the path to a complete reversal of Genesis. In his mind, it is not God who created us but we who created God. In an endeavor to find meaning in the madness of life, we have created a being that is just and right. We have created a being who is loving and kind, who is everything we find lacking in the world we live in today. We create God.

My uncle's specialty is rationology. In those thoughts he is able to explore the rationale of man and all his wisdom. Yet there are moments that the rationale of man goes beyond even his comprehension, and he has to admit it does seem there is something higher than us in the universe, things that the rational mind cannot explain.

It's Just a Little Cough

One Monday my friend Doug had a coughing fit that caused him to pull a chest muscle. He was in quite a bit of pain and went home from work a bit early. On Tuesday night he called to say he was going in for emergency heart surgery and didn't know if he would live through the night. When I got his call I was on my way home with my bride from a Valentine's Day dinner. I took my bride home and headed for the hospital. I, along with a couple of other friends and his family, spent the next ten hours praying, trying to stay awake, and waiting for the surgery to be completed.

He had a bit of a cough, but when he coughed he did not pull a muscle. His aorta had split, and blood was flooding into his chest with each beat of his heart. Most people did not know of this disease, but through the tragic death of actor John Ritter some have heard about it. The doctor let the family know that this was risky surgery and that ninety-five percent of people with this condition die from it. That was actually good news; the reason they die is that they bleed out before they get to a hospital. My friend had a real chance, but the odds were not in his favor. They found a bad valve in his chest as well and found that his aorta was dissecting quite a bit through his system.

In order to properly operate on his heart, they had to put him on a heart bypass machine and take his heart out of his body. The medical community is not as impressed as I am about this; for them it is just a technique, a skill. But through the eyes of faith I am amazed God created us with the knowledge to be able to remove one of our most important organs and repair or replace it. This is a technique and a skill, but for me and my friend, it is also a miracle.

Doug made it through, and when the doctor talked with the family, he said that my friend had been very lucky. The clot that had developed around the original tear in the aorta was the only thing that had kept my friend alive between Monday afternoon and Tuesday evening.

The doctor saw luck, but I knew that the Lord had other plans for my friend and that luck did not hold the clot in place; it was the hand of God. Doug and his beautiful bride are now about to be missionaries in the inner city.

Some people believe the difference between the doctor's opinion on the clot and mine is like Gershwin's song "Let's Call the Whole

Thing Off"—you say toe-*may*-toe, I say toe-*mah*-toe. But I believe for Christians it's much more than a minor difference; it's giving credit and praise either to a chaotic set of happenings, luck, or to the God of the universe. The Lord makes his position very clear: he is a jealous God. He wants our praise and our gratitude for his works in our life.

Let the Worries of This Life . . .

My friend Lee was one of the most creative, funny men I ever knew. He was a Christian performer; he and his partner performed for tens of thousands of people and showed many, many of them God in new and brilliant ways. Lee changed my life. I can't read the Gospels without hearing his voice as one of the disciples. Even as I write this, my tears flow because Lee is no longer with us. Despite all the evidence in front of him, he could not see the facts and truth of God's sufficiency. At his funeral his family and friends spoke eloquently and beautifully about Lee, and it did us all a lot of good to grieve and laugh together.

Over the last decade I had been able to spend time with Lee three or four times a year. I loved and admired him. I think of him and miss him often. The fact that one person can have an everlasting impact on others often escapes us.

If I may take a moment from my train of thought, if you are ever contemplating taking yourself from this world, it is an absolute fact that there are people who love you and will be forever changed, and not for the better. If you are thinking about making that decision, please seek out someone to talk with.

What Lee did, as I see it, is let the world and the things of this world get in the way of the faith that God had for him and all of us. In the parable of the sower, Jesus talks about the different seeds that grow and how they are able or unable to take the Word of God. The first seeds fall on the path, and the second fall on rocky soil, but it's the third group of seeds I want to talk about. If you have heard this parable, you know that the fourth group of seeds falls in the good soil and bears much fruit. But it wasn't until I was forty that I really listened to this parable and realized what the third group of seeds goes through. I always thought that the seeds in the overpowering weeds didn't have a chance. This is how I believe Lee felt. The weeds and thorns of this world were just too powerful and could not be overcome.

But when you read Jesus' explanation, he doesn't say the weeds were too powerful. He says that those sown in the thorns let the worries of this life and the deceitfulness of wealth choke them. For me, the difference is subtle, and I had not seen that before. The thorns did not overpower the defenseless seeds; the seeds let the worries, the deceit of wealth, the world come in and choke them out. They let, they allowed, they went along with the thorns and weeds and let faith go. I realized that is where I had been living my life and where Lee had been living his. It is where I believe most Christians in America live every day of their lives.

The Choice to Move

We don't have to let the worries of this world overtake us. We don't have to let the deceit of wealth ensnare us. We don't have to let the faithlessness of this world take control and let our faith go. We can and do move. No matter where you are thrown, you can move. Unfortunately, that movement can happen in both directions. If you are thrown on the path where the birds can quickly come and devour you, you can move toward the good soil where you experience God and grow. But just because you wish to move does not mean you will. It takes effort, patience, and pain; it takes faith not only in yourself but in the One greater than you as well.

In the spirit of full disclosure, know that you can also move from the good soil to the soil of thorns. You may have been bearing fruit, you may have been in the spirit, you may have had a direct line to God himself, but now you find the lack of money a bit too overwhelming, the responsibility of children greater than you had imagined, the desire to be seen as wise and strong by those around you to be too much to keep this type of faith.

You have the capacity to move from the good soil all the way to sitting on the path, just waiting for the birds to come. Movement by itself is not always a good thing. Only movement in the direction of Christ is always a good thing. Only movement that brings us into a closer relationship with God and strengthens our faith is a good thing.

Anything else is just moving, and just moving is a great way to get nowhere really fast.

Every day God chooses to interact with us. Most of the time even faithful people do not see the hand of God; most of the time I do not see the hand of God. For me it was the hardliners who forced me not to see the hand of God in my life. I do not wish to criticize them or say their actions and words were bad, but as I have gotten older and can reflect with objectivity, it was bad.

I grew up around people who were proclaiming that you were worthless. John Calvin, a reformed theologian, calls this state "total depravity." A person had no redeeming value at all because it was all God, only God. After a few years of this I began to question this theory. If we were truly that wretched, why would this great and awesome Creator bother with us at all? Why would a God who could not even look upon sin look upon us?

Instead of realizing that those who staunchly stated I was despicable and worth nothing to God or humanity were wrong, I assumed that God must not really be active in this world, so I stopped looking for him. Instead of blaming flawed, sinful people for their actions, I blamed God for not stepping in. Instead of realizing these people were simply stating what they had been taught, I blamed God for leaving us to our own devices. Instead of reading the text and discovering for myself they were wide of the mark, I turned to my own wisdom and decided what was right and what was wrong.

Fortunately, God did not leave me to my own devices. He brought people around me who helped me see God and people with different lenses. I realized some good things had happened in my life. My friend Michael fixed my car without accepting a dime, and that was really amazing, because at the time I probably had only a nickel to my name.

My parents gave me love and support, and friends gave me their time and shared their possessions with me. These were not directly from the hand of God, but if God was active in the world, didn't he have a part in it?

These people helped me realize God was not the one creating the wrong perception, it was us; it was me. I came to know people who looked at God with less-dingy lenses and could see his reality a little clearer.

God wants good things in our lives, but for those good things to grow we must have faith and a big part of seeing the good things in our lives. A growing faith has to do with whom we spend the most time. It is no coincidence I met my bride; there were too many obstacles that should have kept us apart, too many things that should have kept us from ever meeting. But we did. It was nothing she or I had done or anything we could have anticipated or arranged. It was God blessing me more than I ever deserved. She is more perfect for me than I could have imagined. I discovered awesome things about her after we had been through three years of dating and then four years of marriage. They weren't awesome because she changed for me; they were awesome because as things came up, the way she responded was perfect for who I was. I didn't know these issues would come up in my life, but she was still perfect. Even now as we approach our eighteenth anniversary, she is more perfect than the day she married me. But back to God's hand and blessings.

Blessings in Disguise

My former college roommate is one of the greatest guys anyone will ever meet. We met sophomore year and spent the next two and a half years laughing together. His bride was my bride's roommate in college. They are amazing people with three children, all perfect for him. One of his children is autistic. It is a condition I didn't know much about, but as I learn more I am amazed how many kids are afflicted with this disability. Doctors told us what to expect when my bride went into labor for each of our children. We did as they said, and we had perfect babies. According to the Centers for Disease Control and Prevention, 1 in 150 children is born with autism. Not once did it enter my mind that our four children would be anything but absolutely healthy. This is not to say that God has it in for parents of children born with autism or cerebral palsy but to say that with so many things that could and do go wrong, it is only by the hand of God that anyone is born perfectly healthy.

I need to step aside a minute when things don't go "normal." A friend of mine has a sister who has Down syndrome. I haven't met anyone in my life who has more joy, more love, and more fun than

Leah. Just because a person is born different or disabled does not mean God is not with them. Sometimes I wonder how much better our lives would be if we lived more like Leah. Just because we are different does not mean we are better. In the case of people with Down syndrome, I believe they have an advantage we haven't figured it out yet.

For the doctors and nurses at the hospital, our children's births were routine. For the grandparents and friends who came to visit, they were special but not awe-inspiring. It wasn't until a close friend told me one of his children had issues that I even considered the blessings from God evident in the health of my children. God was involved in every part of our kids. From the scraped knee that could have needed stitches to the stitches that could have been permanent brain damage. We breathe a sigh of relief because it's not that bad, and we forget it's not that bad because the hand of God was there. The hand of God is with the families of kids with disabilities. God reveals himself through his creation whether we can comprehend the Gettysburg address or not. God reveals himself through the text and those he loves. My college roommate's son may not be able to fix a car, but the love he shows reminds me that even in difficult situations God is good.

Evidence of God's hand is all around us every day if we only take the time to look. We learn from the world to write off God and attribute it to other things, but that is not how the people of the Bible saw it. They attributed almost everything to God including his wrath against people who disobeyed his commands.

We are a nation that sought religious freedom from the beginning. We are a people who say we are "endowed by our creator with certain inalienable rights." We are a people who statistically state that 82 percent of us believe in God (The Harris Poll #90, December 14, 2005). But the same poll shows that 34 percent of the people in the United States believe in UFOs and 21 percent believe in reincarnation. In very many ways our belief system seems to cover several bases to make sure we don't leave anything out. If 82 percent of people in the States believe in God, 70 percent believe in Christ, and 34 percent believe in aliens, that means between 4 and 16 percent of people who believe in God also believe in little green men or grayish men with very big foreheads.

Our faith is such that we have been swayed by the people around us and no longer stand on the Word of God. Because there are some things that are difficult in the Bible, we choose to look elsewhere instead of looking deeper into the text. We choose to take several ideological lines of thought and marry them instead of wrestling with issues and situations that don't gel well with our twenty-first-century American ideal. We choose to water down the very words of God instead of looking stupid before people around us. Our faith has been held hostage by our circumstances.

Compromised Faith

Every day God is performing miracles in the world around us and we ignore them as commonplace or happenstance. Every day we take the faith given to us by the Creator and compromise it with the sensibility of the world around us. All my children have been born perfectly healthy. Not one of them is a prodigy or a genius, and not one of them is deformed or handicapped in any severe way. That is a miracle. To be born in today's world without any defect is becoming more and more a rarity. To be born and have everything work properly is a miracle. When Adam and Eve sinned in the garden, even the ground was affected. Sin does not differentiate between good and bad, people and animals, people and land, sinful adults and innocent babies. Sin pervades every part of our lives, not only our daily lives but also the ground we walk on. Yet when things aren't damaged, we blow it off and don't even think about it enough to call it normal.

We have become so desensitized to God's blessings that when nothing bad happens we don't blink. So often do we see the hand of God in the world that we cease acknowledging it is God keeping it upright. Only when things go terribly wrong do we search our faith. God is in everything we do. I'm not one of those who believe we are absolute wretches and without God we can do nothing. God created this world, and while it is sustained by God, he allows his creation to continue; he even lets us continue denying him.

Faith is assurance in things that have not yet come. Faith is believing when there is by human standards no reason to keep believing. Faith in his Son, in his goodness and in his grace is the gift God has given us to get us through this sinful and fallen world, but so often we begin to do things. In doing things we accomplish stuff, and sometimes we accomplish some pretty cool stuff. When we accomplish those things we start to believe in ourselves. There is a point where we believe in ourselves so much that we can't turn away from the mirror that has become our life. When all we can see is ourselves, we can't see the true Creator. When we eliminate God from our lives and begin to rely on ourselves, we quickly begin to lose faith in anything we cannot see or produce on our own. This is where I believe we live today.

We have accomplished so many amazing things that we cannot comprehend of something bigger than us. But it is not just grand accomplishments we love. In completing those accomplishments we believe we know more than anyone else and so we don't want to take orders from anyone else. We are our own masters. Slavery ended in America in 1863, and we will never bow down to a master again even if it's the Creator of the universe. Our arrogance and independence will be, has been, and is the downfall of our civilization.

Our arrogance has also taught us to look at those who come before us with pity. "Look what we can do" is our mantra. Yet in Jerusalem there is a stone in Herod's temple that is approximately 11 feet by 16 feet by 45 feet and weighs over 600 tons. With all our modern knowledge and material we have just cracked that weight point, and they did it without giant cranes. To suit our sense of self we have not only minimized God's creative work in our lives, we have also diminished the accomplishments of anyone who completes what we can't fully understand.

When our faith becomes so jaded that we need to see a decomposing corpse rise from the dead and grow new flesh in front of our eyes or we won't believe, we have lost our faith. Jesus' accusers asked him for a sign. After telling them that no sign would suffice, he gave them one. "Destroy this temple and I will rebuild it in three days" (John 2:19). Jesus did just that; the temple of his body was destroyed, and three days later was rebuilt. Over the next forty days more than five hundred people witnessed Jesus alive, yet there were people who didn't believe. One of his own disciples didn't believe until he had seen with his own eyes.

Quite often I remind myself of Thomas. I guess I am too jaded and suspicious of the world to simply believe, but that is what we are called to do: believe. Whether we see or not we are to believe, to keep our eyes open for the miraculous and give God the glory. We are to keep our eyes open for the everyday miracles and give God the glory.

There is so much evidence of God and his hand working in our world today that we call it commonplace and refuse to give the credit and the glory to the one who not only created everything but sustains it as well. God's work is all around us, and we could notice the hand of God if we took time to notice the God of the universe.

CHAPTER 5

Justice, Not Just Us

Now go do that voodoo that you do so well.

—Hedley Lamarr

Throughout the Bible are quite a few references to justice: God's justice, humanity's justice, and the lack of justice humans have. Justice for a kid who grew up with *Lone Ranger* reruns was absolutely understood. The Lone Ranger and his trusty sidekick brought justice to innocent townspeople on a weekly basis. He had no ties and no apparent weaknesses. He could bring justice without fear. The Lone Ranger, on his majestic horse Silver, and Tonto, on Scout, rode from town to town in the West, ridding them of bad guys. They never asked for reward; justice was reward enough for these two heroes.

The Wild West gave the best definition for justice a young boy could find. The man with the badge brought justice; he was the only person who stood between innocent townsfolk and bad guys.

The Wild West was around for only thirteen to thirty-nine years, depending on how you measure the influx of immigrant Americans into the West, but this era has given us over one hundred and fifty years of stories, books, TV shows, and movies.

In the Wild West, justice was doled out by a lone man, usually a sheriff or a marshal who stood in the face of immeasurable odds to defeat evil, corrupt men. Some of the great heroes of the early twentieth century were the men who made the Wild West their home, with names like Erp, Wild Bill, Jesse, Buffalo Bill, and Billy the Kid. Good guys and bad guys were idolized and immortalized alike in the search for justice in an untamed land. Justice was dispensed six shots at a time. Justice was not given, it was earned; it was right conquering evil.

But where do we get our sense of what justice really is? What or who defines justice for us? It seems that as we rely on our own wisdom, what justice is begins to change, and not always for the better.

What's Yours is Yours, Unless I Really Need It

In America we have a legal provision called eminent domain, the government's right to take, with payment, private property without the owner's consent. Most of the time this occurs during the building of highways; to build a highway you have to cross quite a bit of private land. Not everyone is glad to see a highway come through, and if the government had to secure cooperation from everyone affected, it would never get built.

The government will assess the lands' worth and buy it whether the owner cooperates or not. For the most part this is an accepted practice no one really minds too much. But in the past few years the Supreme Court has changed the definition of eminent domain. The government may seize private property with payment when the project or need is for the greater good of the community the government is there to protect. But now the Court has given the government the right to seize a person's private property to give the land to a private company, letting it develop that land for their for-profit use, not for public use.

The first place I heard about this happening was on the East Coast, where oceanside homes, actually small, shanty-like homes by today's standards, were being taken so a private developer could put up strip malls and condos. Tourism was down tremendously, and the town was hurting, and this was one of the only ways the town officials thought they could save their town. The people whose houses were being taken were fishermen who had lived in these houses for most of their lives, the same houses their parents and grandparents had lived in. This was their history, their lives, and it was being forcibly taken through a legal definition of the greater good. Who is the good guy here? The man who wants to stay in his house even though the town could be saved if he gave it up, or the developer who wants to save the town and earn tremendous profits at the same time? They both have legitimate points, and they both have legitimate downsides. Is there a good guy and a bad guy in this scenario? How can justice prevail when there is no good guy and no bad guy but two half-right and half-wrong parties?

Let the Abdication Begin

Justice is very different depending on who you are and what you have been through in your life. Justice is also very different depending on what side of an argument you take. We've taken the word "justice" and redefined it to suit our desires. We've taken it, wrapped it up in a bow, and made it a present to ourselves. We've taken it and perverted its original meaning.

Let's consider an easy topic: welfare. I realize the issue of welfare is not an easy one nor will it be solved by the thoughts I have on it, but for this thought process, welfare is very easy to quantify and categorize. If you are a single mother unable to find a job, welfare helps you keep your kids fed, safe, and warm. If you and your spouse are working but have a hard time making ends meet, it may not seem that the government's taking your money and giving it to someone who in turn does not have to get a job is the best use of your money. I'll leave up to the conservative radio pundits the debate about whose money it is, but I don't believe there should be a welfare system. There shouldn't be, but there has to be because of the failings of Christians in America today.

I do not believe there should be a welfare system because one of God's greatest concerns throughout the Bible was taking care of widows and orphans. God is also very specific in including the fatherless among those we are to take care of and look out for, along with widows and orphans. If Christians and the church took their responsibilities from God seriously there would be no need for welfare because the people on welfare would be taken care of by God's hand in this world, Christians. But Christians have abdicated the responsibility God has given them and pawned it off on the federal government. We have taken a biblical command of "so that the Levites (who have no allotment or inheritance of their own) and the aliens, the fatherless and the widows who live in your towns may come and eat and be satisfied, and so that the LORD your God may bless you in all the work of your hands" (Deuteronomy 14:29) and instead said "Well, we pay taxes, and those taxes should take care of them; we've met our obligations."

What we really want is someone else to take care of our obligations and still have the Lord bless us. That is not justice; that is self-indulgence. We give our tithes to the church, which develops programs, gives to missionaries, and builds bigger buildings. "I don't have enough to give extra; let the government take its part and give that to someone who needs it."

It's Just a Jump to the Left

Christians as a whole do not tithe. Biblically, a tithe means one-tenth, but we have redefined it to mean the amount we give to God's work. Christians give about 3 percent on average as tithes. (http://www.herald-review.com/articles/ 2008/01/05/ life/features/1029116. txt) The Barna group (www.barna.org) states that only 5 percent of adults give one-tenth. With those kinds of statistics, no wonder the government has to step in and take care of the poor around us. We are too busy trying to stay ahead of the money curve. We're too busy worrying about what we won't be able to buy or whether we'll be able to pay our bills if we give the amount God requires. We don't care about the poor because we are too busy taking care of our futures. A very wise person once said, "You want to make God laugh? Tell him your five-year plan."

God didn't seem to care about how much you have left for yourself. In Leviticus, God commands the Hebrews not to glean to the very edges of their fields so the alien and the poor may come and glean them. That is very foreign to us here in America. What is ours is ours, and if we want to give, that's fine, but someone should not be able to come onto our land and take something that rightfully belongs to us.

God's concern is not that you get everything you can from what he has given you; his concern is that everyone in the community is taken care of whether by family, friends, or strangers. Widows, orphans, the fatherless, and the poor in your community are to be taken care of by you, not the government. They are to be taken care of by the hands of God, you and me.

We do not share the corners of our fields today. I realize I am pushing the limits of our sensibilities here in America, but in my community the average family size is four, and the average home has 2,500 square feet. Why do we have homeless people in my town today? Four people cannot possibly need that much space. We have homes with thirty-foot cathedral ceilings and sitting rooms bigger than some people's whole apartments. We have so much personal space around us today and yet we don't give away any of it. We keep it nice and tidy for us to feel safe, comfortable, and happy.

I often wonder if we should stop making selfishness okay in the kingdom of God. In America we have made luxuries a good thing. We have made having tremendous abundance a goal to strive for. We have made building up treasures for ourselves here on earth an acceptable, God-sanctioned lifestyle.

Jesus said it is easier for a camel to go through the eye of a needle than for a rich man to enter the kingdom of heaven (Matthew 19:23), but we have tempered that statement to mean *stingy* rich people, those who have money but don't give any away, those with money who are mean about it, those who spend money on themselves and their partying ways, those who have the money we don't. We've ignored the fact that Jesus doesn't qualify the rich in these ways; he simply stated that it was easier for a camel to go through the eye of a needle than for someone who is rich to enter the kingdom of heaven. That could mean only the stingy rich, but it could just as easily apply to anyone who is rich, anyone who has enough that they don't have to rely on God. By the world's standards, this includes most Americans.

We use examples of God blessing people with riches to justify striving for wealth, and Solomon's a great example. He had more wealth than anyone in the world at the time. Some scholars have estimated his wealth was greater than anyone in history, including today. But if you read a bit further in the life of Solomon, his wealth led to his downfall and his complete non-dependence on the God who had given him that wealth.

David went from being a wanted outcast to the ruler of one of the greatest nations in the known world. He was so wealthy he decided to stay home instead of going into battle, and he had an affair with a married woman, had her husband killed, and almost ruined his kingdom. It was only by his humility and his willingness to abandon all he had for God that he was saved. For those thinking a humble heart will save the day, David was saved from the destruction he had put into place, but he did lose his son born from his adulterous union. While he wasn't brought to complete ruin, there was a heavy cost.

A Beanbag Nation

Having money feels good. We are a people who don't like to feel uncomfortable or feel pain. We are a people who coin phrases such as "If it feels good, do it," "I'm okay, you're okay," "If you can't be with the one you love, love the one you're with." In 2005 there were over 6 million children diagnosed and medicated for ADD (http://www.chaada.org/Page3.html). The numbers are staggering on how much we are creating diseases and medications to help manage those diseases. No longer do we get outside with our children and run around for several hours; we now just give them a little pill and a video game.

An acquaintance of mine plays video games. I told him I thought he should get out of the house and spend a little more time with people. He informed me he doesn't spend time alone; he plays his games online with quite a few people from all over the world. This is not community, this is not fellowship; this is a pacifier just as little pills are pacifiers.

I am not pulling a Tom Cruise here and saying medication is always wrong, but I do believe we are an overmedicated society that would choose to have a quick fix rather than the slow task of actually fixing our problems. We don't want to be deprived of anything we desire or wait for anything we feel we deserve. We don't want to be told we can't be rich here on earth and still get into heaven. We have lives to lead.

How can we be personally fulfilled if we spent all our time playing games? When would we be able to accomplish things and be fulfilled? Some Christians say, "We need to be fulfilled; besides, you can't earn your way into heaven. So our actions aren't the root of our acceptance or denial into heaven; our hearts and our spirit determine our eternal fate."

Not so. The book of James is very clear that our actions have a direct impact on our faith. They have a direct impact on what we think, what we believe, and how we follow. Our actions are the indicators of whether our words are full of substance or simply fodder for our own benefit.

Do we seek justice with our words only, or do we seek justice with our words as well as the material blessings God has given us? In America we have tried to have our cake and eat it too and then wonder why we have so many fatherless children; we wonder why the youth of today are so apathetic; we wonder why we have so many overweight people.

Turf Toe, or Something Like That

In the American Christian circles around us today we have taken "justice" and made it "justus." I don't believe we are very different at all from the people of the past; I am sure they didn't see things much differently than we do now.

"Justus" is the term that seems to be infiltrating us once again. Justice is no longer the lone gunslinger facing off against bad guys. Justus is now making sure we are taken care of first, foremost, and fully so we have the lifestyle we have become accustomed to and get into heaven as well.

In Florida a minister and his wife saw a blind man walking with a guide dog in a mall. It was the master's first time out with this guide dog; they were learning about each other and how to get around in society together. The minister's wife saw them coming her way. According to court documents, she did not get out of the way because she "wanted to see if the dog would go around her." The dog did not, and the blind man unfortunately stepped on her toes. Thirteen months later the minister and his wife brought a lawsuit against the guide dog school because the blind man had broken her toe when he stepped on it (http://www.duhaime.org/LegalResources/LawFun/LawArticle-41/ Outrageous-Lawsuits.aspx). This is one Christian's version of justus; she stood in the way to test the dog; when the dog failed the exam, she felt she was owed something—$160,000.

No longer do we look at the whole of our society and seek equal treatment for all; we now look for situations with deep pockets and see how much we can get for ourselves. Justus is me getting mine no matter who else gets hurt.

If the Shoe Fits, Get an Extra Pair as Well

The hard part for me is that this is not an isolated case at all. People who call themselves Christians are daily looking for the quick buck.

Christians are stating things like "If I could just be completely debt free, then I could give my life in service to God." I know a number of Christians who state adamantly that they only want to do God's will as soon as they can make enough money to take care of all their bills and expenses. These Christians play the system and parse every biblical word to help them get ahead financially. Many Christians say that when they have been financially unburdened is when they'll be willing to look out for others. But even when people are given amazing blessings by God that take care of their finances, it's never enough.

I worked in many minimum-wage jobs as I made my way through school. I worked for some nice people and some real jerks. After college I worked freelance in the video and film industry, mostly in documentaries and commercials. I met a tremendous variety of people, some whom I grew to love and some I still love to loathe.

When my bride and I had our first child, I left freelancing and went to work for a ministry that supplied churches with the newest technology in sound, lighting, and video. I thought this was the perfect match; my faith and my vocational passion were finally meeting perfectly. What I failed to realize is that I was going into this line of work completely naïve. I assumed that because 95 percent of our clients were churches I would be dealing with honorable people of tremendous integrity. Unless the Lord directly commands me, I will never work for a business where Christian churches are our main clients ever again in my life. I never saw such absolutely unethical, unscrupulous behavior in my life. These people were not just trying to do the best they could, they were manipulative and mean. They assumed that because they were representing churches they deserved special pricing.

Some of you may agree with their attitude. Of course, in 2006 church and parachurch ministries in the United States reported income of over $92 billion (http://www.scribd.com/doc/1032806/ Worldwide-Church-Income-expenses-and-cost-of-baptism); that's *billion*, and they are yelling at me because they don't have the money.

Just to give you an example of church justus, a pastor came in looking for a wireless microphone for a conference his congregation was having. The church had done a nice job of advertising; I knew about the event. The pastor told me they only had one wireless mic but for this event they were having two speakers answer questions at the same time and asked if I rented mics. Those we had for rent were already booked for the weekend, so I told the pastor I could not help him but knew of other music stores that perhaps could. He declined my offer and purchased a wireless microphone for his event. I had a friend who attended it and told me the question-and-answer time was very insightful and enjoyable. He told me that both speakers had mics on and had spoken at the same time, so everything seemed to have gone well.

On Monday morning a woman from the church that had given the conference came in with the microphone. She said that they hadn't needed the mic, hadn't even touched it. The box had obviously been opened; when I looked inside, I saw that the components had been put back decently but not anywhere as well as the factory put them in originally. She wanted a full refund.

Letter of the Law

When I was in the video world I worked on many different sets in many different roles. I really liked working on meal or food shoots. I got to film food on a table with place settings, good china—the works. It's fun setting up, and the food tastes great once you wrap the shoot. The bad thing is that most of the time you have to buy plates, cutlery, and so on that fit the style you're trying to convey. On the secular shoots I've done this is no problem; production companies buy what they need, use it, and most likely put it to work on a later shoot as well; it's just part of the job. But on almost every food shoot I've done for churches, someone makes a nervous announcement about keeping the dishes and silverware in as pristine condition as possible because they were going to be returned after the shoot for a full refund.

I've never looked into the law to see if filming silverware constitutes using it so it can't be returned as unused, but it is absolutely unethical and immoral. For some Christians, however, justus allows them to do this.

Here are the two worst phrases I have ever heard in Christianity: "I'm not perfect—just forgiven" and "It's easier to ask for forgiveness than for permission." These phrases have been used to justify lying, cheating, stealing, and many other atrocities all in the name of God. They are two phrases that make justus a really comfortable, fun thing, and I would like to see them banned from the Christian vocabulary forever. "Do not deny justice to your poor people in their lawsuits" (Exodus 23:6). "Do not pervert justice; do not show partiality to the poor or favoritism to the great, but judge your neighbor fairly" (Leviticus 19:15).

And a Step to the Riiiiiiiiight

People on welfare deserve a helping hand, but I believe the government should not be the one with the job of taking care of widows, orphans, and the poor because God gave that job to his followers. Christians should be taking care of widows, orphans, and the poor, giving them helping meals in their homes and not on wheels. Christians should be giving them jobs even though it negatively affects their bottom lines. Christians should be giving them places to stay even if it means their kids may have to share a room.

Justice has to have meaning. It has to be rooted in something greater than our own self-indulgence. Justus takes care of the self—first and second; it cares for those who care for us or who can give us money or influence. Justice cares for the poor. Justice cares for those whom God has placed in our lives. God provides justice through us. Not everyone is blessed with wealth; if you are so fortunate, bless God and look for someone in need because there's a really good chance God has blessed you specifically so you'll bless them.

Justice is not up to others; it's up to us. Justice is not the job of corporate or governmental agencies; it's the job of each person. Like the Lone Ranger and Tonto, we are to stand up to the injustice of the world, to the justus of the world, and cry "Stop!" We are to be the justice the world has abdicated its responsibility for. We so often simply write a check, and it's statistically about 70 percent shy of the amount it should be. We so often expect that the paid people in our church will do the work; after all, "That's what we pay them for." But God has called each of us to reach out in community to those around us and help when we can and where we can. Welfare should run rampant, but it should be a private matter from the people of God, not a publicly funded one.

CHAPTER 6

Obedience Held Hostage

It's not in the way that you hold me
It's not in the way you say you care
It's not in the way you've been
treating my friends
It's not in the way that you
stayed till the end
It's not in the way you look or the things
that you say that you'll do

—Toto

God's calls to his children are many. There are over 600 laws in the Old Testament. The details of God's desires for his people are greater and described in more detail than anyone could have imagined if they had set down to describe our relationship with God.

Anyone who has ventured, been coerced, bribed (with ribbons and trophies in youth group) or been forced to travel through the labyrinth of Leviticus knows the pain of God's details. When most fourteen-year-old boys (speaking for myself and those like me) begin reading Leviticus, they are rather excited and intrigued with the heading above Chapter 1, "The Burnt Offering." To begin with, it is the first time we have been made aware that we could use fire, "and God said it was good" (our own ecstatic utterance). Not only do we get to go to heaven, we get to burn things on the way. How cool is that? But by the time we get to verse 9 and read about washing innards, any interest in fire has quickly dissipated, replaced by the realization we've been tricked into reading something no young person was ever meant to read. We weren't even sure old people were supposed to read this boring stuff, but they seemed to, so we guessed it was simply what you did when you got older. This is why Peter Pan and the lost boys gave us hope that we would follow the second star to the right and never have to open the book of Leviticus again.

Not only did reading all the Levitical details set us boys back, all we had was the King James version of the Bible, and here I'm not talking about the New King James, toned down a bit to fit more of the modern era. I'm talking about the real thing with all the thou's, thy's, and sitteth's you could handle.

There are some parts of the King James Bible that invoke glory and honor and are reminiscent of days of old. Its words bring comfort and majesty and invoke a sense of awe and wonder. Plus, half the time you were reading you sounded like a pirate, so that was pretty cool. But you didn't really know what you were saying most of the time, so the temporary joy of adding *arrrggghhs* into the verses wore off rather soon.

As I read the words of God now, I see this is where it all began. This is where the law, that which the people used to follow God justly and rightly was born, at least for us. This is where God created his nation, where God began his relationship with his chosen people.

These are not words that drone on and on. These are the very words of life. These words *are* life. I don't know if as a fourteen-year-old I could have fully understood that, but looking back I wish I would have been trained in the right way, the Christ way, to try to see it as more than droll on the gold-edged pages.

That's It

That's where true obedience begins for me. What does it mean to obey? Do we obey because we want to? Do we obey because we have to? Do we obey out of the reformer's sense of guilt, grace and gratitude, or do we obey because we don't want to get on God's bad side?

That was it. That was my life. That was the life of most people around me. That is how we lived. We didn't obey out of love for God or out of gratefulness for the lives we had. We obeyed out of a sense of fear and duty. We didn't want to get on God's bad side. We loved him because he first loved us. We were to behave a certain way because he was God. We were to do and be because if we didn't, we'd go to hell. I realize some of you are stopping in shock and disbelief, saying, "I've never felt that! I believed because of who God is, not because of what might happen to me." For that I praise God. I hope you never know a day when you feel your obedience is obligated, when your obedience has been held hostage by the circumstances of your life. I hope we all can come to a place and say, "I believe and I obey not because I have to but because I choose to." But as I look at the believing world, there are more people for whom obedience is a chore and a burden—fire insurance rather than a joy and a privilege.

Obedience to God, to anyone for that matter, takes on different looks depending on who's obeying and what the landscape of his or her life looks like when the call to obey comes. Most of the time, in twenty-first-century America, obedience comes in the form of not hurting other people. We have made it an art. The "I'm okay, you're okay" generation has made a credo out of doing what feels good; as long as no one else gets hurt, they're fine with their actions. They obey what they believe to be the right thing. Hurting someone is not right, so that's become the litmus test, but the other moral issues they face are strictly subjective.

Who you are and where you are in life are the important determining factors in deciding behavior, not a set of philosophies or guidelines imposed by someone else (like "the man," using the sixties vernacular). Obedience is a societal tool when it protects others. From speed limits to taxes, we enact rules to protect people from others on the road and to help those who need a little assistance. But God's call to obedience rarely involves other people. Let's take a look at the rule of obedience most people think of when they first begin to think of laws: the Ten Commandments (Exodus 20:2-17).

> You shall have no other gods before me.
> You shall not make for yourself an idol.
> You shall not misuse the name of the Lord your God.
> Remember the Sabbath day by keeping it holy.
> Honor your father and your mother.
> You shall not murder.
> You shall not commit adultery.

You shall not steal.
You shall not give false testimony.
You shall not covet.

While murder is obviously a case in which someone suffers, the other commandments are more innocuous regarding pain. The emphasis on these rules is you and your relationship with God and others. "You shall have no other Gods" is a statement of belief and doesn't involve anyone else.

The same is true for commandments two, three, and four, which deal with your relationship with God—that's all. While at times we band together and in a community go against these commands, God is calling us individually to follow these regardless of others.

Honoring you father and mother is at worst uplifting and gracious and at best dutiful and respectful. Honoring your father and mother is the only commandment that carries a promise of blessing. It's about relationship with one another; it's about caring for God's community.

While stealing can sometimes be hurtful, one could easily rationalize that "They had so much they don't even know it's missing," and the self-justification litmus test passes with flying colors. Giving false testimony against your neighbor may be telling a lie to get that neighbor in trouble, but it could just as well be lying to get someone out of trouble. Surely helping my friend can't be wrong, but Scripture doesn't say that we should be truthsayers only when it helps. We are not to bear false testimony under any circumstance, even when it can help a friend. We are to be truthful, period.

Coveting is internal and may never involve anyone else. If you notice, I skipped one: number 7. While most people see committing adultery as harmful, there have been trends throughout history (and today's society is no exception) that committing adultery is not harmful. In fact, some proclaim that the act has actually saved their marriages. There are sections of today's population that state vehemently that having more than one sexual partner is what keeps marriages fresh and make them last longer. While most people like me scoff at such a statement, the people who make it most of the time have been married longer than their pastors or elders.

A number of polls taken around 2000 put the divorce rate at 27 percent. That stat is for "born-again" Christians. It was roughly 24 percent for other Christians. Now on one hand that's a good stat in comparison to media reports that Christian divorce is close to 60 percent, but this poll also found that 21 percent of atheists are divorced (www.religioustolerance.org).

Grace—Really a Cheap Excuse to Do What We Want

My sense of humor is such that I really want to crack a joke here about how Christians beat atheists at everything, even divorce, but just sit back a moment and let that reality sink in. We have bought into the world philosophy so much that even though the Bible makes it clear we should work it out, we have ignored God's command and have followed society's lead.

We are supposed to put personal desires aside and work together to keep our vows alive. We are to believe the person we are with is someone God has brought to us and wants us to be with as we grow and change to be more in his image. "But we have grace!" (Say all of this with a sarcastic accent). "We don't have to stay in loveless marriages anymore. We don't have to settle for someone who no longer looks like a twenty-year-old sorority girl. We don't have to be shackled to someone who doesn't let us do what we want when we want."(Now back to your regular non-sarcastic accent.)

Grace, a wonderful, amazing gift from God, is also used to justify and rationalize some of the most blatant sins humanity has ever committed. We have bought into the philosophy that God wants us to be happy, so we leave our wives to "find ourselves" with women willing to let us be happy. This is what obeying our own desires and not God brings about.

Just so I don't alienate all the men messing up and calling it good, I'll mention a new trend in vocational religion today. Women are leaving their husbands, destroying their families, and pursuing their own selfish agendas all in the name of God. Wives (not all or even a majority, mind you) are leaving husbands to become pastors, breaking one of the most sacred vows to follow God's call. I don't know to what extent they truly believe this or are just using it as a great excuse, but they say God told them to make this move. They use God to destroy husbands, to wreck their children, to go after positions of authority.

I'm not talking about or arguing about women in ministry; this is not about that. It's about women claiming to be obedient to God and following him by destroying their families. The most horrifying thing to me is that seminaries are welcoming these women with open arms.

Paul is clear that men are not to be elders if their families are not in order, but we have seminaries accepting and ordaining women whose families are in disorder because these women want this authority. We have disguised power as obedience and have claimed it in God's name so no one could argue, and we've gone down the path of destruction no one's willing to stop.

While this isn't directly related to adultery in the most literal sense of reading the text, Jesus in Luke 16 tells us if you if you divorce your spouse and marry another, it's adultery, no exceptions. It's easy to criticize the motives and actions of some men who take newer, younger wives, but women leaving their husbands for "ministry" reasons are no more acceptable in the sight of God.

Sex and sexual acts seems to be one of the most flexible "obeys" that society has. The pendulum of acceptance with sex swings further than most things we as a people tolerate in any other category. By some estimates the pornography industry made over $13 billion in 2006. This is not an industry supported by only loose-moral singles and lowlifes. For the industry to get to $13 billion, there must be plenty of Ward Cleavers out there who aren't using pop-up blockers.

One nationally known pastor recently came out about his gay lover and his meth use. Sex is the one thing that seems to affect more people than any other sin. To quote George Michael in his song "Sex," "Sex is natural, sex is good: not everybody does it, but everybody should." That has become the mantra of our society, our credo and our life ambition. It has become what we desire and what we should want. It has become our god.

The Ties that Divide

What we are called to obey varies even between Christians. Most commonly this is called dogma, which has been responsible for more fractures in the body of Christ than any other item, and I'll bet it has been responsible for more brokenness and separation within the church universal than all other issues combined.

I came from the Reformed tradition. The reformation was without a doubt a good thing that, I believe, placed us back on a path closer to God. But in looking at just one of the offshoots of the reformation, I don't know if the reformers would have chosen to begin the reformation if they could have seen the divisiveness within just one segment of the faith community.

This is a small denomination within the denominations that call themselves Christian. They all began with the same parental unit. But as doctrine or dogma was established, some felt that certain things could be lived with while certain things could not. In an effort to seek truth, both sides let it escalate until a rupture occurred and division was born. In the name of obedience we fight, mock, and kill. In the name of obedience we denigrate, trample, and derail those we are supposed to call brothers and sisters. In the name of obedience we condemn, threaten, and denounce those who hold different views, shouting proudly that we have the truth and that others are just blind to what God has called us to.

The phrase I use to encapsulate this theory is, "There but for the grace of God go I." I have watched Christians justify hate, condemnation, and pride using this phrase more than any other. I once heard a woman say about other Christians who didn't believe as she did, "If it wasn't for the grace of God, I would be a wretch going to hell, just like them." In her mind she was praising God for showing her the light, but if you dissect that statement, she condemned someone to hell for not believing the same things she did. She took it upon herself to pass God's judgment for him. She believed what God believed, and if you didn't see that, you were just a sorry, hell-bent person not worthy of her time. And we wonder why there is division in the body of Christ.

Rev. Vander Laan leads teams of people through biblical, historical journeys in Israel and Turkey. He takes his groups to a Roman temple now in ruins and tells of the temple's former beauty and majesty. He then has you look at the ruins, the final remnant of scattered, broken stones that were the temple. He ponders aloud if this is what God sees as he looks down from heaven at his church.

What does God see when he looks down on us? Does he see a body trying, thriving, and being light in a darkened world? Or does he see remnants of stones thrown down by battles long fought, no victor standing? Unfortunately, in the church today are more tossed remnants than there are bodies standing. We have taken obedience to a whole new level of killing. In recent times we have seen extreme Islamic groups bring to light the depth of pain and hurt obedience can cause. But the church has more victims of its obedience than all the people who boarded planes on that September 11.

In Christian terms I am speaking largely to the church, the bride of Christ, those who have been part of and established the institution whose sole purpose is to bring the love of God into the world. We have failed at this point and failed miserably.

We have used the obligation of obedience to keep the wayward in line. We have used the obligation of obedience to keep our children and those we care about safe. And in some cases, we have used the obligation of obedience to keep our power.

The church is not evil; it's the bride of Christ that is and shall remain the instrument God uses to reveal his kingdom in and to this world. But the church is the body of believers. The church is the community of people gathered in faith to praise and worship the one true God. The church is not the institution of brick, mortar, and dogma that humanity throughout the ages has established; it is precisely the people, the body of Christ in that institution who have caused us to stray from true obedience to God. We as a church have caused people to stray into the area of cheap grace.

When I Googled to see what other people were thinking about obedience to God, I was utterly amazed that with all the websites that came up on the search, all the advancements we have made as a society, one of the key principles in Christian faith, obedience to God, is being denigrated by cheap grace. The people behind these sites were honestly trying to help others better understand faith, but they missed the mark for the sake of numbers. We have made Christianity easy. Not that Christianity is necessarily hard, but it does take a lifestyle change to walk the path of God. We want people to come to Christ, but we know if we ask too much they won't begin the journey. So we dumb down the Christian faith and leave obedience to God at the door of souls saved.

A number of years ago I was really into television evangelist shows. People who watch those shows wonder why we aren't reaching the new millennium generation, but it's bad TV at its best. I love bad TV. I love shows so awful there're like passing a horrible accident: you desperately want to look away from the carnage but you just can't. One night one show was bringing in its big donors. The hosts were stating how much money it cost to run the show and how many people were saved as a result of the show. One donor gave a check for tens of thousands of dollars. The dollar amount, according to the show, was enough for 10,000 people to come to God. He handed over the check and said with orgasmic glee, "Those 10,000 souls are mine."

I believe he was stating that his efforts were bringing 10,000 people to the Lord and that the Lord would give credit to his efforts for those lost souls being found. The Bible reveals to us that no matter what you—an individual—do, it cannot bring someone to the Lord. The Lord initiates faith; he makes others receptive to the call of God. The Lord puts us in the honorable position to be in the right place at the right time to witness someone coming to faith in God, but we have nothing to do with that; the only credit we receive is being receptive to the Lord and following his call. But saving souls appears to be what most of the modern-day church is about. Wherever you live, if you are not actively attempting to bring people to Christ, you will be asked, "What are you doing if you are not saving souls?" You will be pushed, bullied, and manipulated into saving souls because that is what God's call is all about: saving people.

Oh, wait; I thought the great commission was to make disciples. To get people to say they believe in Christ, make a disciple, same thing right? No, absolutely no, without hesitation or reservation no.

Definitions Lost

Jesus made disciples; it took him three years, and according to most rabbis I have read that was a pretty fast timeline. We are to make disciples, not create a league of scared converts who will go back to their way of living after they get fire insurance. We are to be concerned not with numbers but with the community God has placed us in. Sometimes that means growing, and sometimes that means numbers. But numbers are the by-product, not the goal, of good discipleship.

Most churches will state publicly that the number of attendees is not among their top concerns, but the truth is that for most of them the number of people in pews and the offerings they bring in is very important.

When is a church dead? When it's completely empty and even the pastor isn't showing up? In most cases it's when the number of people in the seats is insufficient to cover its costs. It may still have dedicated members, but financially it cannot sustain itself and therefore is deemed dead and closed.

The irony is that this isn't the case for many churches. With endowments, a large church can keep going in absolute irrelevance while the denomination keeps funding this dead, lifeless body. But in many cases, if the funds are not there, the church does not stay open. So to keep numbers up we alter what we say a little bit from the front, not enough to be heretical but enough to keep people who want an easy life and a free ride coming and giving.

The websites I found on obedience were mostly from a New Testament perspective, but they didn't know or observe the truth of the New Testament at all. One lengthy site stated there were only two things that needed to be done to obey God: "Love the Lord your God, and love your neighbor as yourself." This site went on about how we didn't need to obey or even know the Old Testament laws anymore because of Jesus. What? We didn't need to know or obey the Old Testament because of Jesus? He *inspired* it. He *was* it. He was the Word. These were his words, his law. Not only did he originate it and inspire it to be written by the Old Testament writers, on earth he memorized it. He lived it. He knew it as a human. He studied it. He learned it. He quoted it. These were words of life for Jesus. The words "Love the Lord your God and your neighbor as yourself" don't eliminate the laws of the Old Testament, they fulfill and complete them. They uphold them with righteousness and faithfulness. To do these two things you have to adhere to all the other laws, for if you love God you'll obey all his laws.

This is not an exhortation on each law and why it should be observed. Each law has its place and its context; they point to that which we must obey, but it is a heart of obedience that matters. God's law will always stand regardless of humanity, time, or modes of transportation.

The Standard of Holiness

What comes and goes is obedience to God, the following of his Word, the living out of the life he's called us to. What is the life God has called us to? I believe each of us has one overriding call of obedience that is the same for all of us; it may manifest itself differently, but it is one call. We are called to be holy as God is holy (1 Peter 1:15).

People in general want control and power. They want to be in control of their lives, of their destinies, of their situations. In an ironic twist, God made people his church. While the church is the bride of Christ and all the glorious and good things that go along with it, it is also people with all their flaws, problems, and sins.

A friend of mine was growing in a church; he and his bride were heavily involved in many areas and outreach programs. While they were a bit unconventional, they were doing good work for the Lord. The leader of one outreach program was someone who wanted respect and power, but he didn't earn it, he demanded it as the appointed leader who was to be obeyed. It is amazing to me how many times the "authority" sentiment is expressed within the church. Unfortunately, the Bible is often used incorrectly and/or out of context to support the leader's control. This leader made an accusation about my friends, and the senior pastor simply accepted his word. No questions were ever raised about the accusation; he was a leader, and so it must have been true. The senior pastor had put this leader in the position and trusted that this leader was a good man. My friend and his bride were asked to leave all they had given their talents and their lives so freely for, so they left the church. Not just that church. They left the Church.

A few months later it was discovered that that leader who had made the now-known-to-be-false accusation was also committing a whole host of sins. He left that church and is active in another part of the body that doesn't know his history. For my friends, the greatest hurt was not the accusation or the initial belief in the leader who made the accusation; it was that when the truth was revealed and the deceptive leader was asked to leave, nobody made any attempt to reconcile with them. The senior pastor may have thought that his control would be lessened if he admitted the deceit and thus decided that this couple would just be lost in the fray. Fortunately that is not the end of their story with God, because he has more patience and love than any of us.

Holiness is not something that needs power; it is usually the opposite of power. Being obedient to the holiness of God usually means being a servant to all.

Obedience is a good thing in the right hands, but it can be used for pure evil when in the wrong hands. The other day, some film-buff friends of mine and I got into a discussion of "bad guys." We each had our favorite bad guys and agreed for the most part the best bad guys were those who smiled at you while they did horrible, evil things. We agreed that one of the most insidious characters was played by Tim Roth in the movie *Rob Roy*. He wasn't Jason or Freddie; he wasn't even Darth Vader. He was small, meek, but absolutely evil. Evil doesn't always have horns and fangs; sometimes the most evil thing can masquerade as something most innocent. Sometimes disobedience to God is masked in the light of true obedience.

One of my favorite producers/writers is Mel Brooks, who has created some of the best and funniest movies in the history of film. In most of his films Mr. Brooks makes hysterical fun of anything and everything. In his movie *History of the World, Part 1,* there is a great bit on the Spanish Inquisition. While writing this, the lyrics "the inquisition, let's begin, the inquisition, knock out sin" are happily going through my mind. It is a masterful sketch that shows what happens when power and people run amuck. The inquisition is something very few people I know of even acknowledge must less take notice of. It was a time when the church, in obedience to God, did some of the most sinful, horrific things in the history of humanity. While the movie version is very funny, the real version is not.

> Millions of innocent people were tortured and murdered during the inquisition. The inquisitors followed procedures set forth by the Dominican monks of Pope Innocent III. At first the poor accused were told to confess. They were then stripped naked, shaved, pricked with needles for insensitive spots and then examined for marks of the devil. Before the torture started, the victim was told what was about to happen, and in many cases this forced the accused to commit to whatever the inquisitors wanted. It was noted that a person

who refused to talk even under torture was being aided by the devil. While the poor victim was being tortured, a clerk recorded what was said. In many cases the clerk recorded things that were not even said. Each subsequent round of torture was much worse than the one before. The torturer was paid out of seized funds belonging to the victim. If the victim had no money then the relatives were made to pay. While the poor victims screamed with pain the childish tortures carried on like sadistic maniacs. They sprayed their instruments with so called holy water, wore amulets, herbs and crossed themselves. The exact method of torture varied from place to place. The rack was well used in France during the inquisition.

Some victims were horsewhipped. A sharp iron fork was used to mangle breasts. Red hot pincers were used to tear off flesh. Red hot irons were inserted up vaginas and rectums. A device named the Turcas was used to tear out fingernails. After the nails were ripped out needles were shoved into the quicks. Boots called bootikens were used to lacerate flesh and crush bone. Thumbscrews were used to crush the fingers and toes. Acid was poured on victims and hands were immersed into pots of boiling oil and water. Eyes were gouged out by irons. Alcohol was poured on the head of the poor victim and set alight. Water was poured down the victim's throat with a knotted cloth. The cloth was then jerked out tearing up the victims bowels.

There was no limit to the types and cruelty of the tortures. The inquisition meant anything was allowed. The inquisitors were sadistic and mentally disturbed. Even after the poor victims confessed to things they never did more torture was to follow. On the way to the stake or gallows victims were flogged, burned, branded and had their hands and tongues hacked off. By the 17th century as the Catholic Church began to lose power the inquisition began to collapse. Millions had died as a result of the inquisition, including men, women, children and babies. (www.paralumun.com/ inquisition.htm)

"The road to hell is paved with good intentions." The worst cases of abuse regarding obedience were started with good intentions. These men were trying to be obedient to the church and their own sense of righteousness and power, but they saw it as obedience.

People don't generally start off being tyrants. They develop that skill over time and with the grace of power. Most people require obedience so that organizations, families, etc., can run smoothly. You obey your boss not only to keep your job but because usually he or she knows more than you and can see a bigger picture than you can. You don't get into the cleaning supplies because Mom told you not to even though at age three you don't know why you can't.

The Hippie and the Marine

A good friend of mine is a former marine. Marines are a unique breed; they obey orders unquestioningly. Marines are not made, they are born, and then the marines within are revealed through training. One of the biggest "discussions" we've had is about obeying orders. He believes, as any good marine does, that you carry out orders to the very end. You obey orders whether you agree or disagree with them. Even after seeing Germans shooting at you on D-Day, your orders were to take that beach, so you did.

There are a lot of good things about being that driven, and I along with millions of others thank God daily for those with the ability and desire to carry out orders and keep us free.

I was raised by two hippies. My parents wouldn't qualify as complete hippies because their faith kept them from experimenting with sex and drugs, but in every other way they were hippies. I question authority on every turn; I don't follow blindly when leaderships' competency is in question.

My marine friend is an optimist; I'm a realist. He believes that God is good and will prevail; I believe that man is essentially selfish and will seek out his own self-interest in spite of his word, honor, or loyalties, and that while God is good, he doesn't usually stop man from being the self-centered egocentric creature he is.

I purposely chose the word "man" and not 'humankind." Women have the ability to be just like men at times and fight more ferociously than any man I've ever seen. If you ever doubt that women are ferocious, just ask any man if he would ever step in the middle of a chick fight. But most women I've met are more concerned with relationships than power positions, and this creates a much more honoring and grace-filled life.

I believe that my marine friend and I each have significant points that help our argument. I also believe that in the end people who do not truly desire to "be holy as God is holy" will take the power and authority they've been given and abuse it for personal gain. This is never truer than in the church.

I have met many people in my short life but never anyone (while I am sure they exist) who rejects or hates God because of God. When I have talked with people who hate God, they point out how Christians have sinned, have turned blind eyes, have given harsh judgment and graceless correction.

A man I know is one of the most amazing people I have ever met, and I'm honored and proud to say he is a friend for whom I'd do anything. I named my son after him. He wants nothing to do with God. He's smarter and more talented than most people I've encountered. But when I look in his eyes I see a man who is longing for God. He yearns for greater meaning than himself or his creations. His soul is crying out, "I want to believe in something that's real; I want to believe in something that's true. I want to *believe*." But he sees children being abused by religious leaders; he sees women put down and degraded; he sees gay men and women ridiculed and beaten because of how they choose to express themselves; he sees people of faith condemning others while hiding behind religious doctrine and calling their sins God's true will. They consider their faith a "members only" club others aren't good enough to get in unless they repent and begin to think just like them. And if those others don't choose to think like them, they'll use their power and position to beat them down. This is what my friend sees when he looks at the institution we commonly call the church. This is not God; this is not Jesus Christ; this is not how we are to be; this is definitely not how God wants us to be seen.

Rejection 101

When I first became a Christian, I took part in evangelism training and learned many very helpful things. Though there were suggestions that weren't really me, I saw how they could be adjusted to my personality. I also heard words of comfort in the face of rejection. But those words, I've discovered, while well intended were false. Anyone who has taken a training session on evangelism may have heard this comfort disclaimer: "If you approach someone to share the Good News of Jesus Christ and are rejected, don't be discouraged. That person isn't rejecting you but rejecting Christ." While that reassurance emboldened us, I've come to believe it's not true. If people, including my friend, ever met Jesus, they would not reject him. Those people are rejecting us. They are rejecting what we represent. They are rejecting who we are identified with: other Christians. All too often we represent the church instead of Christ, and that is what they reject. We are acting and representing the holiness of the church rather than the holiness of God.

So what is the holiness of the church versus the holiness of God? To answer that I believe we need to look at the life of the Rabbi we are called to follow. He calls on us to obey all of the law, and we can do that if we fully obey the greatest two. "Love the Lord your God with all of your heart, mind, and soul. This is the first and greatest commandment. And the second is like it: Love your neighbor as yourself. All the Law and the prophets hang on these two commandments" (Matthew 22:37-40).

A theme that seems to pervade history and cross cultural barriers is that being good is an attribute to strive for. In the Hellenistic culture, if you were good, the gods would look down upon you and see your works and reward you appropriately. In the spirit cultures of the North American Indians, you treated the things around you well so you would not offend and anger the great spirits watching over you. Even those in cultures that don't subscribe to higher powers show concern for how they will be remembered by those they've left behind; eternity or the afterlife for them is measured not only by how many people remember them but also what they're remembered for.

The world has recently seen the ultimate distortion of this belief in a small, radical segment of Muslims who were taught to believe the best thing they could do is die for Allah. But dying was only a small part. If in dying they were able to kill as many "infidels" as possible they would be greatly rewarded. They were being good soldiers of Allah by obeying the call to eradicate anyone who didn't follow the call of Allah. These people were not born hateful; they did not look around and decide the world was so evil that they needed to leave it and take down as many others as possible. These were people trying their best to obey the commands they had been taught. In their minds they were no different than a young woman who went to live and care for the poorest of the poor in Calcutta. They were no different from the preacher who led a march to Selma that landed him and others in jail. These people are just obeying what they have been taught.

In His Name

Those born into the generation X era have let the past be distorted a little and don't remember this type of justification has happened before. On September 11, 2001, thousands of people died because of others' obedience to Allah. Between 1933 and 1945, over 6 million Jews were murdered in the name of God. I say in the name of God because part of the whole reason given for the annihilation of the Jews was a biblical interpretation in the name of Christ. Through hindsight we look at Hitler's record of death and destruction and proclaim proudly that he was not following God, but in the name of Christ, Hitler and those under his command slaughtered millions.

In the name of obedience to God people are able to do almost anything. In one Monty Python sketch, a couple of men are just sitting and talking when the Spanish Inquisition breaks through the door screaming, "Nobody expects the Spanish Inquisition." While their robes and accents make us laugh, the truth behind the comedy is that in the name of God people were brutally and mercilessly tortured.

Just to see the tools used brings winces of pain and shock. People were tortured in the name of Christ. They were stretched on racks, hung by their thumbs, burned, cut, and beaten in the name of Christ. We are able to say now that these people were demented and distorted and did not represent Christ or his bride. But at the time this was believed to be an act of obedience, in his name. In the name of obedience men marched across the European continent and killed many people to reclaim the Holy Land. The crusades were one of the bloodiest wars the world has seen and it was carried out in the name of obedience.

People seem to be willing to do almost anything in the name of obedience, but obedience doesn't always mean hurting or murdering others. In the name of obedience the Essenes left behind the rest of the people of Israel and went off into the desert. In the name of obedience a young Christian couple left for India to take care of lepers and spent the rest of their lives caring and advocating for them. In the name of obedience a young Olympian full of potential and hope refused to compete on Sunday and endured the shame of a nation.

Obedience is not just about sacrifice, but when compared to the expectations of the world it can come across as one. Obedience comes in many forms and expresses itself in many languages. But the root of the question I propose is why do we obey?

Why Not What?

I grew up in a very conservative, religious area in which we all knew what we believed, but why we believed also meant something. Statistically you have a 95 percent chance of believing things your culture teaches. If you grow up in the Midwest, you most likely believe octopus is not to be eaten raw, but if you grow up on the Japanese island of Hokkaido, it's a food you most likely love. If you grew up in the Middle East, using your left hand to eat is offensive and wrong. I'm a lefty, so when I was thinking about taking a trip to that area, I practiced eating with my right hand.

Obey, as defined by Webster's, is to carry out the instructions or orders of; to carry out (an instruction, order, etc.); to be guided by; submit to the control of [to obey one's conscience].

While I believe we all need to be objective, we are all influenced by where we are from. I am a male from the American Midwest who came from a middle-class home with two parents still married and still very much in love with each other, their children, and now their grandchildren. That is the world I understand. I never had to obey a parent who was drunk, as friends down the street had to. I never had to obey a command from my father to lie about his whereabouts, as some kids I went to school with did. By many measures I led the all-American, 1950s life. We are all flawed and scarred by the fall. Sin creeps in our life long before we realize it's there. It grabs a hold of us and uses us long before we can comprehend the consequences and pain that accompanies that sin.

Our culture can never be completely erased from our being. And that is a good thing. My friend David, a Kenyan, and I see things quite differently on a few issues. I've come to realize that there are a couple of things I should begin to look at through David's eyes and that there are a couple of things, now that he's living in America, he should look at through my eyes. But most of the things we see we should see as we do. We are different. We bring different gifts and ideas to every situation. We should keep and honor each other's differences. But being follower of Christ, we have a greater call to alter what we think and how we live to be obedient to Christ.

CHAPTER 7

Words

Strange voices in my ears
I can feel the tears,
but all I can hear are those words that never were true
spoken to hurt nobody but you

—The Monkees

Living in America today is an interesting dichotomy of purposeful meaning and meaningless purpose. In the words of the greatest superhero team ever, "You must conquer your fear or else your fear will conquer you" (The Sphinx, Mystery Men).

Following in the Greek tradition, America has chosen a language that is very specific. In our culture, specific words have specific meanings. Those meanings can change over time, and they can also become a parody of themselves such as when a big sister states loudly that she could "just kill her little brother." We know these are just words of frustration; while the word "kill" might match the emotional turmoil her brother is causing, the actual act of killing isn't in her mind or of those listening. For the most part, however, we are a literal nation of laws made up of words. Those words can be used to build up, tear down, glorify, or humiliate. Depending on the context, the same words can build or destroy. Depending on your political affiliation, they can be words of comfort or words of destruction. Depending on what team you root for, they can be words of condemnation or words of "rebuilding for next year." (Just ask any Lions or Cubs fan.)

Quite often though a word can become so large and so usable that its true meaning becomes mired in ambiguity. Fad words that have come and gone in my lifetime include "groovy," "awesome," and "phat." As

Snoop Dog and other rappers have proven, there is a vernacular, a new set of phrases out there I am completely out of touch with other than to know they exist.

Depending on your culture and your influences, i.e., when you were born, where you were raised, and who you hung out with, a huge number of factors contributed to your language and your understanding of word definitions. When I was a teenager, my crowd picked up the surfer's name for a very good looking girl, "Betty," while our code name for a homely girl was "Jane." Now that I think of it, I had two girls in my class named Jane, and both were very attractive. I didn't know anyone named Betty other than my aunt, so these names were not based on anything but the devious minds of fifteen-year-old boys. When one of us said "there goes Jane," we all knew what he meant.

Buzz Lightyear, Ruth Buzzi, and Busby Berkeley— It's All the Buzz

Many other words have meaning for each of us but lack simple definitions. Most of the time they are used in situations that don't have a great impact on our activities, but occasionally we stumble on a word we like, and we begin to own it so much that the word becomes a feeling and not a connotation. It ceases to become a word of description and becomes a statement of empowerment, a buzzword. Businesspeople and politicians use buzzwords more than most of the people I've encountered. In the 1980s, one of the buzz phrases I heard a lot was "trust but verify," which is the height of irony, because where there is trust there is no need for verification.

A business-world buzzword is "empowerment." It takes on many different meanings and is used too often. One of the key buzzwords in the institutional church today is "freedom." It's a word most of us understand, one that we've heard going way back, one that invokes more of a feeling than an actual definition. Most of us know what the word freedom emotes in us, but very few of us have the same definition for it. Words similar to "freedom" that Christians tend to use quite a bit are "love" and "forgiveness." We know these words when we hear them but cannot define them because they encompass a vast array of meanings.

All You Need Is Love

I love football (especially the Green Bay Packers), I love my children, and I love Peppino's pizza. While I use the same word for all three emotions and assume most of you can relate, it does not possess the same meaning or the same definition in these different cases. My love for my children is unconditional, my love for Peppino's pizza is conditional upon the recipe, and my love for the Packers is less than the love of a person but more than the love of a pet, but in each case love is there.

Not one person I know would say that my love for the Packers is the same as the love for my kids. We say we love our favorite sports team, and we say we love our kids, but we don't mean the same thing with those two statements.

Christians, at least in the Midwest, Protestant circles I grew up in, used the biblical phrase "we love him because he first loved us." They use it a lot. It's a phrase in the Bible that says more than I could ever fully comprehend. It says more that any human could really comprehend, but we like how it sounds, and we like how it makes us feel, so we say it—a lot.

But what does it mean to love God? We say he loves us, and as evidence of that we point to the wealth we have and the air we breathe. We say God's love is any good thing we have in our lives. I don't disagree with that, but with the notion of free will it is possible that God did not want us to have some of the "good" things we have. He felt we would be better if we didn't have so many possessions or so much free time on our hands, but with free will at play he allows us to bring into our lives things we believe are good whether they are or not. We don't really know what God's love means, so we attribute it to a variety of things.

Love is a good thing in our culture, and so we call the good things in our life God's love. We can't say this is for certain, but it makes us feel better. Then there is the second part of the equation, us loving him. Though I have been a Christian for just over two decades, I still don't have any idea of what loving God truly means, except to quote Jesus:

> If anyone loves me, he will obey my teaching. My Father will
> love him, and we will come to him and make our home with

him. He who does not love me will not obey my teaching. These words you hear are not my own; they belong to the Father who sent me." (John 14:23-24)

Even if you are a biblical literalist who believes this verse gives the exact definition of what loving God is, it is up to interpretation as to what "obey my teaching" means. For some it means going to church every Sunday; for others it means keeping the Ten Commandments; for some it means openly accepting gays into their communities; for others it means holding those people God has brought into your life to a higher standard. No one definition is right, and no one definition is wrong; they're all subject to our personal places in life and our interpretations of what it means to love.

It is similar to the wonderful bracelet movement in the early nineties, What Would Jesus Do? It has inspired both faith and sarcasm, and rightly so for both. It is not a phrase or word we can grasp, but it makes us feel good.

Love is all over the Bible and all over the world. It is a word that has been beaten to death by people to make us think they are talking about something that has greater meaning than it really does. Jesus said there is no greater love than laying down one's life for your brother (John 15:13). If that's the greatest example, what do we call it when it's not so serious but it does mean more than "like a lot"?

And a Happy Bowl Day to You Too

A good friend of mine loves the University of Michigan and college football, so on New Year's Day we are always in his basement along with a dozen or so of our friends for Bowl Day. In Holland, Michigan, New Year's Day has been changed for one small section of the population; just as Seinfeld had a "festivus for the rest of us," it's a happy Bowl Day here. We set up as many as seven televisions and catch all thirteen to fifteen hours of action while eating chili and cornbread.

My friend gets understandably excited when the University of Michigan gets to the Rose Bowl. I remind him that Michigan has been to the Rose Bowl nine times and has won only three times, but that doesn't matter to him. He loves that day, he loves that game, and he loves the U of M. He roots for Michigan every year they make a bowl game, but most of the time he is disappointed. We love our dogs, we love our families, we love our favorite movies, but none of those uses of the word "love" has the same definition or holds the same connotation.

While words have specific meanings in today's world, they don't have that much power anymore. In the novel *The Scarlet Letter,* the red letter "A" on someone's dress meant something. I am not endorsing that type of social shame, only pointing out this letter's meaning in that context. In today's world we say quite a bit and all the time. During election times, a tremendous amount gets said by both sides.

This year my oldest daughter is old enough to understand most of the political commercials coming about now, in 2012. She asked how one ad could say something about a candidate and then another ad say the opposite. I told her that it's accepted in American politics today for candidates to lie. They lie about their records and what they'll accomplish; they lie about their opponents and what their opponents will accomplish. They don't call them lies because of the probability that some of what they are saying they'll accomplish could come true. Regardless, in the political realm candidates lie to get elected.

According to Divorcerate.org, America's divorce rate for first marriages is 41 percent, for second marriages 60 percent, and for third marriages 73 percent. In all the weddings I've been to or heard about, "till death do us part" is part of the vows the couple promises each other.

Given the statistics cited above we definitely don't take that "until death" part very seriously; even though we know exactly what we mean when we say those vows, we don't hold ourselves to them down the line.

My Kingdom for a Bowl of Soup

Unlike our easiness with letting our words mean little, God is not the same and neither were the people of the Bible. When God says something he means it, and it cannot be changed.

When Esau had come home from a long day, Jacob's food smelled so good that Esau sold his birthright for the food. If I ever tried to make such a bargain, everyone would know that once I got the food I would take back my birthright and would have been shocked if my little brother tried to actually enforce the deal. You don't get an entire birthright for a bowl of stew, I don't care how good it is. But in that time and that culture the stew wasn't the cost of the birthright, the declaration was. It's not that the stew was worth the birthright and so the deal was equitable, but Esau's words cemented the deal. Once he ate the stew, his birthright was gone. It was no longer his because his words were set in stone.

When Isaac was dying and wanted to give the Lord's blessing to his oldest son, he sent Esau to kill the animal and make the meal so they could celebrate the blessing together. Jacob got there first and put goat's hair on his arms and the back of his neck and put on Esau's clothes to fool his father (whose sight was very bad in his old age) into giving the Lord's blessing to him instead of Esau. Jacob lied; he was just a schmuck of a person who stole Esau's blessing. When Esau found out what had happened, he said what every one of us would have said: "Bless me—me too, my father" (Genesis 27:34).

But Isaac was not able to give a second blessing of the same kind. Even though he and Esau realized Jacob had deceived Isaac, the blessing had been said and could not be changed. The part that Christians don't usually talk about in our society today is that even though Jacob stole the blessing, God honored it. He held up the words that had been said.

When Joshua led the Israelites over the Jordan River into the Promised Land, they were approached by the Gibeonites, who had a plan that was a lie. They fooled the Israelites into an alliance (Joshua 9). When the Israelites discovered the truth, they knew they had to honor the deal or lose the favor of God even though the Gibeonites had lied to them. They had not sought God's wisdom when making the deal, but they had to honor what they had said, to live out the words they had used.

Jesus told his disciples after the resurrection, "If you forgive anyone his sins, they are forgiven; if you do not forgive them, they are not forgiven" (John 20:23). I haven't heard a good discussion on either side that this command is only for the eleven disciples or for all Jesus' followers, but in either case, for the people involved this was a great responsibility.

Imagine having the power to forgive or not forgive and knowing that God will forgive that which you forgive and not forgive that which you don't. But what if you're in a bad mood and want to be self-indulgent? Doesn't matter; if you don't forgive, neither will God. Our words will bring someone forgiveness or condemnation. We like to think God is bigger than that and will see we are fallible people who make mistakes and forgive those of us who make them, but that is not what the Scriptures say. God will live up to our words. If we forgive someone, they will be forgiven. But if we are being stubborn and mean and refuse to forgive, God will not forgive them. He will hold us true to our words.

The Dishonor of Self-Integrity

In today's world we don't see our statements as set in stone. No longer do we honor our word if doing so doesn't helps us; we honor our word only if it is in our best interest or if the law forces us to do so. "I promise" means "I will—if it fits into my plans and if it still makes me happy" or "I will—if it fits into my schedule and isn't too much work."

Starting in the early 1800s, the London Stock Exchange's motto, "My word is my bond," is revered to this day but not necessarily followed. That phrase came from transactions that happened so fast there was no time to seal them with the proper paperwork. All you had when you made the deal was the integrity of the person with whom you were dealing. Unfortunately, people realized they could go back on their words, get rich doing so, and find others who would trust them because these others want to be rich as well. Self-gratification has made our words meaningless and worthless; though our words have specific definitions, they don't hold the weight they would if we had integrity and honor.

Free as a Bird Loose in a Box

Freedom calls up in us certain feelings and historical memories. Depending upon the part of the country you are from and the cultural setting you were raised in, freedom has different meanings. For my friend the marine, freedom is something he takes very seriously. He is from a military family; his father and grandfather had served in the army, and he proudly served in the Marines to secure freedom for all Americans. The unbelievable men and women who serve in the armed forces know what freedom is and what it costs. They have seen firsthand in the Middle East that freedom can deliver people from oppression. They know what freedom feels like, tastes like, and means.

Because I'd grown up with hippies, guns were neither part of my upbringing nor part of my culture. Freedom in my culture was freedom from "the Man." Freedom was a right you had, not something you earned. Freedom was from God (or whatever higher power you could conjure), and you had the right to have it, and it was (to quote my earliest language instructors) *groovy*.

I believe that both definitions of freedom are equally valid and that God has given us freedom to choose what we want in this life, hence the choice to eat of the fruit. I also believe that the "feelin' groovy" generation got it wrong: because of sin, freedom is not free. There is a cost associated with the freedom we experience in America whether in battle, in court, or in a classroom. Freedom is the right to disagree and do so vehemently. We can limit and even deny freedom to others. To get what they want, dictators over the generations—Castro to Hussein, Genghis Khan to Hitler—have limited people's freedom. Throughout history people have tried to get the freedom they want even if it meant oppressing others to get it. Benjamin Franklin once said that "[t]hose who would give up essential liberty to purchase a little temporary safety deserve neither liberty nor safety." The desire for freedom was the core of this country's beginning, but sin is the core of all men. Because of sin our selfish, power-hungry natures have the freedom to grow and to be unleashed on society.

Forgive Us Our Deb . . . No, Transgressio . . . No, Sin . . . No . . .

"Forgiveness" is another word the world uses quite a bit and Christians use even more; it is abundant in the sermons of pastors and the speeches of politicians. Forgiveness is what we have been given, and forgiveness is what we should give in return.

We are to forgive people's transgressions, or debts, or sins or . . . It gets so confusing when we change the official script, but nonetheless we are to forgive.

But what does that mean? What does truly forgiving someone look like? Merriam-Webster defines "forgive" in this way: "to give up resentment of or claim to requital for; to grant relief from payment of; to cease to feel resentment against (an offender)." To cease to feel resentment against—is that all it is? There's nothing more involved? To cease to feel resentment against? What then? To cease to feel resentment against? Is that what it means to really forgive? What if someone does something bad? If someone steals your wallet or purse but you get it back, you can cease to feel resentment against that person. But what if you don't get it back? What if you don't know who took it? Can you cease to feel resentment against someone you don't know?

Let's say you cease to feel resentment against someone you don't know for stealing an object from you. What if that person took a person from you—your father, your mother, your child? What if that person took your dreams, your virginity, your life? Does that person get the same forgiveness as the one who stole your bicycle or your wallet?

Let's take it a little further: consider people who didn't kill or rape anyone, they simply abandoned you when you needed them. How far does forgiveness go when they're family? A good friend of mine is the child of divorce. He was entering his teen years when his dad left, and though he occasionally met with his father, for the most part his dad was not a part of my friend's life. He is now nearing midlife, and his dad wants to have a relationship with him. The father has never apologized for or owned up to the damage he caused when he abandoned his family. So what does it mean to forgive? Does forgiving mean no longer feeling resentment against someone? Does it mean beginning a relationship again? How far does the definition of forgiveness go? Is my friend obligated as part of forgiving to have a relationship with this man who abandoned him? While each of us knows how forgiveness would feel if we were in his situation, I don't believe the actual definition or the look of that forgiveness would be the same for any two people.

Free to Be You and Me

I'm taking a step back to talk about freedom again. Freedom is much like forgiveness in that we understand exactly how it feels to be free, but I don't think the definition, the "look"' of freedom, would be the same for any two people.

The first time I heard a preacher talk about freedom was in a charismatic church setting full of energy and excitement and a little bit of bouncing. The pastor was almost screaming, "Don't you want freedom? Do you want to be free?" The questions made me pause. Did I want freedom? That was an interesting question. I live in America; I'm free. Aren't I? If I'm free, why is he asking me if I want freedom? What does he mean when he says "freedom"? What does freedom mean to me? Do I want it? Freedom from what? Freedom from whom?

I don't remember a bit of what he said after that point because I was very preoccupied with the notion of freedom and what he was really asking. Do you want to be free? Do I? As I thought about the proclamation of freedom, I thought of some things it could mean; some things I know this pastor would not want and would never say I'm free to do. Was I free to run around this sanctuary naked? No, I didn't undress in the sanctuary. I just wondered *Am I free to run around here naked?* King David did, and even though he was King, there were complaints about his actions. How can I, a middle-aged, middle-income white guy be free enough to dance before the Lord naked? Not only am I not Brad Pitt, I'm not even in normal, television-person shape. It would not be a pretty sight. But this question, do I want to be free? still ran through my mind, so I began to dwell on it.

Am I free to shout anything I want in Christ's name? In my life there is a current discussion happening regarding language. When I was in high school, an English teacher told us we could not take the Lord's name in vain in his class, but no other appropriately applied language was off limits. One of the more brazen students raised his hand and said, "So I can say whatever the f@#? I want and it's okay?" We were stunned: he just dropped the F bomb in school. We knew the proverbial poop was going to hit the fan. The teacher looked at the student and said, "If it is appropriate to the subject you are dealing with, yes."

We were even more astonished; the teacher had just let the student get away with saying an obscenity in class—no pink slip, no detention, no punishment. What was going on?

Back to the present day. Do I have the freedom to say words that aren't even in Scripture but are obscenities by today's cultural standards? Do I have the freedom to say other words? What does freedom really mean to a Christian?

I don't think the pastor or anyone in that room really wanted me to have complete freedom; most people want you to have complete freedom to do what they do and think what they think. We take a reverse-Pauline philosophy on freedom. Paul stated that we were to not use our freedom to cause others to stumble. If someone has an issue with things to eat, we are not to flaunt what we can eat but to humbly join and eat only what our brother or sister in Christ would eat so as to not cause them to stumble (1 Corinthians 8:13).

What some have done is say, "This is what I believe is right, and I think you are not in line with the 'true' interpretation of God, so you should refrain from what I refrain from and have what I have." We have taken Paul's words and turned them from a subservient act of freedom to a controlling act of comfort. We deny others freedom so we can feel free, but Christianity is about a different type of freedom. In fact, in one sense Christianity is the complete opposite of freedom. Paul describes himself as a slave to Christ yet proclaims there is freedom in Christ. Christians follow the path of Christ. Being a Christian does not mean being free to live however *you* see fit. In Christianity, you are free to do whatever you want as long as it fits inside God's law. That pastor would not allow me to have an affair or abandon my responsibilities to my children or run naked through the sanctuary during the Sunday morning service, and for all those things I am very grateful.

But just as with "love" and "forgiveness," a vast array of meanings comes with the word "freedom." I don't believe we are to abandon the word, but I do believe we need to find a way to use the word properly and find other words to describe the feeling or situation we are referencing.

Freedom of Clarification

What I believe this pastor and many others in the world of Christianity are talking about is not freedom but release, a form of freedom. I don't believe these people are completely off of the mark, but we aren't talking about freedom to do whatever we want; we're talking about freedom from oppression, from domineering authority, from the demons haunting our lives. In every sense of the word we are talking about freedom, but freedom is too wide of a net to throw out over an entire congregation.

Not all of us sitting in that building are under those types of oppression. We do not all need to experience freedom in those areas. Being a white, middle-class male in America, I haven't been subject to a lot of the oppression others have had to endure. Does that mean the pastor should not talk about freedom because some of us have not had to endure social evils? By no means, but by simply asking the question "Do you want freedom?" we begin to trivialize the word and make it a popular buzzword that no longer has meaning but makes people feel good and like the person asking the question.

Does Anybody Really Know What Time It Is?

In different times and cultures, languages develop with different nuances. Our American system is based on the Greek/Hellenistic way of life. By that I mean there are some cultures in which the concepts of language and time are very loosely defined; just because you say it doesn't mean you mean it.

I've had the privilege of visiting some Latin American countries. Entering a non-American culture is an amazing learning experience. I was on a video shoot, and our guide said our next interviewee was going to meet us at 1 p.m. In the American video world, time is a precious commodity and schedules are very important, but we learned that in Latin American countries time is not quite as exact as it is here in the States. When it was 1:45, our producer was getting very annoyed, but the guide then told us that 1:00 did not mean precisely 1:00; it could be anytime between 1:00 this afternoon and tomorrow. Our American sensibilities were torn; in our culture 1:00 meant 1:00, so how could he be late? We got over it, but we did learn a lesson about our culture.

In Greek-influenced worlds words mean things, and those meanings are very important, so much so that a former president actually said in the midst of a huge sex scandal, "it depends on what the definition of 'is' is." Are you serious? Politicians throw out phrases and accusations like old men throwing crumbs to ducks, and one was parsing what the word "is" means?

It's good and bad that in American culture words mean things. On the good side, when we say something, a definite image and meaning comes with it. On the bad, definitions can sometimes be so broad that two people can come away from a talk with two entirely different interpretations of what had been said. Using phrases that sound good may make for good presentations, but when the presentation is a sermon, I believe we need to provide a bit more context to make sure we aren't just throwing out God slogans to make our sermons more popular.

If It Sounds Good, Say It

Just recently I was looking at a Christian school's sports handbook. With good intentions they stated that their athletes must exhibit "Christian behavior," a phrase we use in various contexts that doesn't say what it means. The person who wrote that sentence most likely knew exactly what he or she meant by Christian behavior. But as we asked in our discussion about freedom, what is Christian behavior? In most traditional Protestant worship settings, lifting your hands above your shoulders and shouting "Amen" to the Lord is not outlawed but is definitely frowned upon. But in more independent and charismatic churches, singing with your hands in your pockets or with your arms folded is often seen as a sign of repression, a sign you need to be "released in the Lord." The Bible depicts people living their lives and God blessing them along the way. That must be what they are talking about by Christian behavior.

But wait; among the main people in the Bible are a murderer, a liar, a thief, a prostitute, an adulterer—and I'm just up to Chronicles. The behavior of these people God seemed to bless, love, and call to lead cannot be called Christian, but God still chose them; he still blessed them.

Our traditions and history have cultivated our definitions and meanings as much if not more than our faith and our text have. We throw out Christian terms as if they are universal terms for righteousness, forgiveness, and sin, and we expect others to live up to our ideas of what they do or don't mean.

In modern American society words have become hooks on which we hang all our stability. We have become a society of lawyers and legalese. We have become a people who say one thing and then change or encompass additional meanings into our words to get out of what we've just said. We are a people who like to throw out phrases that make people feel good but don't really do anything to change our lives. "Do you want freedom?" "Change we can believe in," and "Read my lips" are all slogans that are part of our consciousness, that make us feel good, that have meaning for us. But they mean something a bit different for everyone listening. You can't tie a rope around them and get a hold of them. You can't define them and therefore limit them. You can't hold them up to scrutiny and denounce them. For businesspeople and politicians these words and phrases are invaluable and effective, but Christians have to be very careful not to fall into the same trap of superficiality.

The text is very clear that words have power: "Reckless words pierce like a sword" (Proverbs 12:18); "[A] deceitful tongue crushes the spirit" (Proverbs 15:4).

Any adult in therapy can tell you the biggest lie adults have promulgated on children is the phrase "sticks and stones will break my bones but names will never hurt me." Cuts and broken bones heal, but the pain from hurtful words can last a lifetime. Our words are so precious; shouldn't we guard against hurtful statements and make sure our positive statements are not just empty war cries to rally the troops? Our words should really mean something.

CHAPTER 8

Your Own Bootstraps

These boots are made for walking, and that's just what they'll do.

—Nancy Sinatra

Throughout our lives we all grow up with one thing in common: heroes. Whether it is Superman, Daredevil, a fireman, or your dad or mom, we all have heroes we look up to, emulate, and strive to be like. The interesting thing about heroes is that they are almost always solitary figures who take on the world by themselves. Oh sure, Batman had Robin and the Green Lantern had Kato, but it wasn't about the sidekick; it was about the hero. Real-life heroes didn't seem too common in my life, but as I've learned through stories and movies, there were real-life heroes around me and I didn't know it.

The only stories I'd heard about World War II came from staying up way past my bedtime and watching *Hogan's Heroes*; what I "knew" about the war itself was that Germans were incompetent fools and Americans and their allies were heroes who saved the day again and again.

The adults in my life never talked about war stories. They would mention almost in passing that an uncle or a neighbor was there on D-Day, but they never said what that meant. I'm not sure they knew. Men who lived such experiences don't often talk about them freely. In time, some people began to tell their war stories, but they aren't the stories we expect to hear; they weren't of people who stood in the face of danger and saved the day with X-ray eyes or superhuman strength; they were of average men in incredible situations who had to rise to the occasion or die. Not one rose to the occasion every time; not one had all the answers. Individually they often didn't see a way out, but together they leaned on each other and helped each other get through some of the worst conditions and most horrifying sights anyone has ever seen and conquered one of the most evil dictators ever.

They were a team. They were a community. Closer than brothers, they lived and died trying to save each other. When you go to war, you go for country; when you fight a war, you fight for the man beside you. The bigger picture doesn't enter into it much; you're just trying to stay alive and keep the men and women around you alive. No superheroes swoop in to save the day, no special powers or trap doors let you escape from danger quickly; it's just you and the people around you: it's community.

When the dust and the tickertape settle, we forget that lesson. When the parades conclude and people started living normal lives again, stories of heroic feats remain, even grow with the telling, but tales of community fade into the background; the stories of brotherhood, the backbone of the success, get lost. When we honor individuals who were "responsible" for the great victory we miss the target. By that I don't mean we got everything or even most of it wrong. To the contrary; most people get more things right than they get wrong.

Realize that when we do goof up, we do it very well; from slavery, and open drug experimentation to new-wave music, when we mess things up we do it big. But we also got to the moon, we discovered the sequence for DNA, we invented Twinkies. What every generation since America's beginnings got wrong is the American ideal of pulling yourself up by your bootstraps.

Good and Right

From its conception America has been known as a rugged place of strong individuals. The first Republican woman was chosen to run for vice president not too long ago; it was a historic event not only because Sarah Palin was a woman but because for the first time in quite a long time we had someone running for office who is an absolute individual. She is the very definition of a rugged American. She did not come from privilege, and by that I mean wealth. She did not come from a political dynasty as did the Kennedys. She did not play the system and work her way through the ranks so that she was "all the buzz." By just being who she was she got noticed, people became impressed with her, and they followed her. In very many ways she embodies what is good and right about the American rugged individual.

Matt Damon made some comments about Sarah Palin, and his questions of her competency may or may not be justified. Everyone has the right to research presidential candidates. But what bothered me about Damon's comments were not his slams of Sarah Palin, nor his rip on Disney (though I am a huge Disney fan, so that stung a little). My concern with what Damon said was his anger and venom toward the ideas that the earth is only 10,000 years old and was made by a creator. If believing that there were dinosaurs here 4,000 years ago is one of the litmus tests for being in politics, then our political system is in trouble.

This feeds into our bootstrap mentality. Damon is a man who has pulled himself up by his own bootstraps. His fledgling career was saved by a script that he and Ben Affleck wrote. But his hate and anger for those who believe God created the world as it states in the Bible amazes me.

Jesus said that people would hate us on his account. According to other statements made by Damon and films such as *Religulous* by Bill Maher, people who believe in God are simpletons who should be pitied but not understood, distrusted but definitely not followed.

I realize that a great number of Christians have bought into the millions and billions of years thing for the earth's age, and I'm not debating either position here. What I am saying is when a more conservative view of the Bible is now seen as not only stupid but also dangerous, I wonder how long it will be until belief in a God at all is taunted and discriminated against in a country founded on religious freedom.

In America we have freedom of religion, not freedom from religion. We weren't put on earth to get as much as we can, to be that solitary figure who rides in and saves the day. We were put here to be a community of believers who lift up, assist, correct when necessary, and always love each other.

Since its declaration of independence from tyranny, America has fueled the dreams and imaginations of people around the world who lived under systems in which their places were not determined by their own efforts but by those of their parents and grandparents. Individual efforts and determination did not allow people to achieve their goals; rather, it was whether they had the right connections. But in America you could be whatever you desired to be. While the statement doesn't hold as much power and respect as it did when I was in elementary school, in America you can still grow up to be president.

We see most candidates doing and saying whatever it takes to get elected and even going outside the law in a few cases to get or keep that power. But even though we don't give it much weight in today's society, being the ruler of one of the strongest nations in the world is pretty awesome. There have been some amazing American men and women who have risen despite all odds and made history.

The Hidden "I" in "Team"

As we began to memorialize great individuals of the past, we have also created a juggernaut that's taken on a life of its own. No longer did a band of men cross the Delaware and turn back the British on Christmas Eve; now, George Washington crossed the river and beat the British. So much so that in Bucks County, Pennsylvania, a town along the Delaware River was named Washington's Crossing for that event and the man who led the team.

As Americans we don't particularly like teams. In football we have our teams, but within that team structure we have individual players, "our" players we really root for, the ones we tune in to see win the game for our team. When our star players are traded or retire, we immediately look for the next superstar on our team. And if we can't find a superstar (being from Michigan, the Lions have provided many superstarless teams over the years), we create personal hype about a particular player's potential, and when he doesn't deliver the "greatest in the world" image we've built up, we lament that fact (or being a resident of Michigan).

Some smart people gave up on the Lions a long time ago and became Packers fans. Okay, that was just me. Even though Favre is no longer a Packer, the Packers are still the most awesome team in the history of the NFL, and Aaron Rogers could be one of the greatest quarterbacks ever.

We don't want teams because then we can't have heroes. Michael Phelps is, in my opinion (along with many, many others) the greatest Olympian ever, having won eight gold medals in the 2008 Summer Olympics. But only five of those were individual golds; the other three were team medals. Granted he was on those teams and definitely contributed to their success. I was a swimmer in school, and while I was never even close to the caliber of Olympic swimmers, it is still in my blood, and I love the sport dearly.

In the 2008 Olympics were two of the best swimming races I've ever seen. One was the one-hundred-meter butterfly that Michael Phelps won by a hundredth of a second. That was amazing, awesome, but not in my opinion the greatest race of those Olympics. For me it was the four-by-one-hundred-meter relay. Michael Phelps led off and did very well. From the start the lead teams were ahead of the world record, and by the middle of the race it looked as if the top three or four teams would all break it. When the last swimmers dove in for the final leg of the race, the U.S. swimmer was behind by almost a full body length. Right then the commentators were giving the U.S. the silver and questioning Phelps's race for seven gold medals in one Olympics, done only once before in history by Mark Spitz in 1972.

As I watched the last swimmers hit the wall at fifty meters, I was somewhat resigned to getting the silver. But Jason Lezak, an old man by Olympic swimming standards, was determined not to settle for less than gold. As he came off the turn he gained on the French swimmer. I remember saying out loud that I didn't think he had enough time to beat him. There were only about twenty-five meters left, and France looked strong. But as they got toward the end, something amazing happened. It was as if someone was picking Lezak up and throwing him forward as he stroked. He was gaining. It was the most amazing come-from-behind swim I'd ever seen.

Lezak ended up swimming the fastest one-hundred-meter relay leg ever: 46.06 seconds. He came from behind and beat the French swimmer by eight one-hundredths of a second. Those of us really into swimming will remember Lezak and his incredible finish, but if you check the papers and the headlines, Lezak may get a quick mention, but the other two swimmers, Cullen Jones and Garret Weber-Gale, have been left behind as the unnamed "team" because the conversation is about Phelps.

Since it's still in reruns, I'll assume that everyone reading knows about *Gilligan's Island*. These seven stranded castaways were also a team. We knew them from the theme song that played and played and played in our minds after hearing it just once. But in the first season all seven of them were not named. The Professor and Mary Ann were given the shaft by just being "and the rest." In our society it is about the star; be it Michael Phelps or Bob Denver (Gilligan), we don't like to have teams to root for, we want "the" guy.

It's okay to have a few people surrounding the principal character; occasionally they'll get a little notoriety, but all in all we want the star. Another example includes two television shows in the 1990s. *Friends* and *Seinfeld* were arguably the two most popular television shows in television history. Their ensemble casts worked truly well together. But as people talk about these shows today, only one or two characters shine in the hearts of loving viewers.

We like *Magnum P.I.* Sure, Rick, T.C., and Higgins were in almost every episode, but it wasn't enough—we remember Magnum. Even *M.A.S.H.,* in my opinion the greatest TV show ever, had some great actors and an amazing cast; as great actors left, they were replaced by other very talented people, but Alan Alda stands head and shoulders above the rest. We love the perky sidekicks, the loyal few who stay with the hero through thick and thin. Samwise Gamgee is a hero to every *Lord of the Rings* follower, but it's really about Frodo, isn't it?

Cullen Jones, Garret Weber-Gale, and Jason Lezak will hopefully not become Olympic trivia, but most likely we'll not hear their names again unless they rise by themselves to accomplish something we can brag about. Their team gold will go down in history as a Phelps "and the rest" gold because we like the idea that one person can beat the odds, that one person can do the impossible.

That is not, however, the way God intended it to be. In fact, when you look through the Bible, it is when a person is trying something without community that things seem to fall apart.

A Community of One Doesn't Work

God looked down and saw Adam and said it was not good for him to be alone. God created a spouse, for Adam, but I find it interesting that God walked with Adam in the garden before he created Eve. Adam was not alone; God was with him.

Plus, when God said it was not good for Adam to be alone, he had already created the creatures of the world. Adam was surrounded by life, but that wasn't sufficient for God. He had made us in his image; we were not meant to be solitary individuals who didn't need a community of people. We were created to need each other just as we were created to need God.

Even God had a community around him. In Genesis, when creating the world as we know it, the Bible quotes God: "Let us make . . ." Let us? But this is God. Then we read over and over about the heavenly hosts. The accompaniment of angels that God has around him is amazing. But even with all that, with the Trinity being in place from the beginning, with the heavenly hosts around God doing his bidding and singing his praises, God still felt the need to create humanity, a relationship he desired to have.

God calls us to be in relationship with him and with each other. Because of our free-will choices, that call quite often gets us into trouble. It is not God leading us into trouble; our sinful nature seeks out the same in others, and eventually trouble is at our doorstep. But we are to be in relationship nonetheless; we are to be in community with each other.

In the Gospels Jesus tells the story of the prodigal son. If your Christian upbringing and teaching was like mine, the Prodigal Son did not make good decisions. Sure, he took what he was entitled to but didn't spend it wisely. He spent his money on prostitutes and wine. What a sinful thing to do.

The adults I listened to as a kid made sure we knew the Prodigal Son's mistakes and that we were not to do the same. That was the story I got; that was the story we all received. I went through junior high and high school and was not told differently. I went to a Christian college and wasn't told anything different. I went to and graduated from seminary and was not told there was anything else to the story. It was the story of a son's sin and father's forgiveness. But after I was out of seminary, I heard an interpretation of the story that blew my mind. The interpretation was that the sin of the Prodigal Son was not in his actions after he left the family. Of course he would fall when he left the family; how could he stand alone? The Prodigal Son's sin was in leaving his family, his community.

It is expected in American culture that sons and daughters take what is theirs and leave the family when they come of age. We are Americans, individuals. We don't want twenty-eight-year-old sons or daughters still living off Mom and Dad. But in the historic Jewish context you didn't leave family. You stayed and helped each other. You were an integral part of life in your family. Close family was the only thing that kept you alive.

They had synagogue and such but not the relief agencies we have today. They didn't have welfare systems or meals on wheels; they had only each other. They were supposed to stay and take care of each other, so they just didn't leave.

The Prodigal Son's sin was not what he did once he reached his new destination; his sin was turning from God and thinking he was smart and strong enough to create his own destiny.

In this same way the sin is not in our actions after we leave; actions we take after we leave are inevitable because no one can stand alone. The only way we can stand against the temptations and pressures of this world is by standing as a community. We need a community—whether it's two or two hundred—to stand.

All for the Want of a Toe

"So that there should be no division in the body, but that its parts should have equal concern for each other" (1 Corinthians 12:25). To stay with my football analogies, this verse, for me, is best exemplified by football players. Football is a game of strength and endurance, most of all a game of hitting and running. Football players do amazing things every week of the season that I, a mere mortal, just sit and admire.

Every once in a while you'll find amazing athletes whose strength, speed, and endurance is unmatched in the game. As I was watching a game, I saw that one superstar wasn't at his best. He didn't have a concussion, a torn ACL, or a broken arm or leg. His big toe was hurt. His big toe? Here was a guy who'd take horrendous hits and get up, throw the ball to the ref, get in the huddle, and do it all again. During the game, the announcers read a list of several players who were out at the time because of toe injuries.

The Apostle Paul knew what he was talking about. All members of the body should have equal concern for each other. Even a great athlete can be brought down by a toe. The same is true for us as a society. There are people in the group who are the brains or the heart or the arms; everyone has a place, and if we leave someone out of the mix because he or she seems as insignificant as a toe, it will affect the whole body.

A Day to Remember

Years ago, when my best friend's son was two, we were at a mutual friend's house watching football with a large group. The son, Jed, was walking around, looking a little scared at all the people. They weren't strangers, but they were many. I noticed him by the kitchen and thought I would hold him to make him feel a little bit better. I walked over to him, held out my arms, and asked, "Hey bud, you want to come here?" He looked at me and smiled. Just then another friend came over with a ball. Jed loved balls, and at age two he could throw better than most five-year-olds. The friend bent down and asked Jed, "Do you want the ball?" Some other people noticed my friend and me and joined in, each grabbing something to entice Jed. Eventually there were four or five of us in a competition: who had the best enticement for this two-year-old? My group, while friendly, considers everything a competition. We were all calling to Jed, but all I had was me. Since I started it, I'd come unprepared. I didn't have the ball or a toy or candy. I thought candy would have been brilliant, but because I didn't have it I decided it was a bit underhanded.

After about fifteen seconds Jed looked at each thing and chose. He came running straight into my arms. Jed and I had been hanging out a lot that year, and he chose me. He chose our relationship over things; he chose someone he knew loved him over the temptations around him.

Children have an amazing way of teaching lessons without trying. Almost two decades later, Jed is now in college and a man after God's own heart, a man of tremendous faith, and still one of my dearest friends. Jed doesn't remember that day, but I'll never forget it.

Choosing community and the love of people who truly care about you is a lesson that we should not take lightly or for granted once we learn it. Pulling ourselves up by our own bootstraps has nothing on a two-year-old choosing you over a ball or candy. God showed me more in that moment than I had ever learned doing things by myself.

We have been created to be together, to need each other. Because we have been created to be part of a whole, even the least member of that whole can have a tremendous impact on our lives and our direction.

Challenge Issued

In the second year of King Nebuchadnezzar's reign, he has a dream. He calls his wise men together—actually, his father's wise men. He has been on the throne only a couple of years and is still feeling his way around having absolute power. The king tells his wise men he has had a dream, but he wants the wise men not only to interpret the dream but tell him the dream itself. Why he does this is truly up for grabs. The Bible never gives the actual reason Nebuchadnezzar makes the wise men tell him the dream and the interpretation, and there are many different thoughts on this.

My idea is that the new King has questions about his father's people. While there is no direct evidence for this, my best guess would be that as he grew up, Nebuchadnezzar heard some of the back-room talk and mumblings about his father's wise men. He may have even heard his father question if the advice he got from the wise men was truly wise or just in their own best interests.

Nebuchadnezzar gives them the challenge of relating and interpreting his dream and also the consequences: "This is what I have firmly decided: If you do not tell me what my dream was and interpret it, I will have you cut into pieces and your houses turned into piles of rubble" (Daniel 2:5). The American Standard Version of this text reads, "I will have you torn limb from limb."

> Though some Bibles use the phrase "cut into pieces," the Aramaic does not refer to cutting instruments . . . The punishment was to be "torn limb from limb" which probably referred to a form of punishment where the victim was tied hands and feet to four trees. When the binding holding the trees together was unloosed the trees would fly apart, ripping the body into pieces. (http://www.pytlik.com/observe/daniel/narratives/ch02-1.html)

When the advisors can't answer the King's request, the commander of the King's guard is dispatched to kill all the wise men. The text implies that when he got to Daniel, Hananiah, Mishael, and Azariah, they did not know about any of this; men simply showed up and said they were sent to kill them.

Daniel talks the guard into giving them a little time to seek an answer from their God. As a community of four, they pray that God will answer their prayer and save them from death. God answers their prayer, and they're saved, but not because one person is really insightful or smart. They rally as a community of believers, working together so God might be glorified.

Even when Daniel relates the dream and gives its interpretation, he does not take credit or see this as an avenue to put himself into a better financial or status position. For Daniel, it's about glorifying God. He realizes that alone he can do nothing, that alone he is unworthy of approaching God and asking for help. It is only as a part of a greater community of close relationships that he can discern the wisdom of God and accomplish anything meaningful.

Drawn Together

"A new command I give you: Love one another. As I have loved you, so you must love one another. By this all men will know that you are my disciples, if you love one another" (John 13:34).

I have heard it said that you are never closer to someone than when you face death together. As the four Israelite friends face a group of soldiers wanting to kill them, they draw upon each other. They gather not only for themselves but for the glory of God as well.

God is able to do anything he wants, but he seems to choose not to do some things until we initiate our faith. God knows what the dream is. I believe that God gave Nebuchadnezzar the dream. God even knows, unlike Daniel, that the king made this request. God could have easily just given Daniel the dream and the interpretation without any problem, but he waits until Daniel, Hananiah, Mishael, and Azariah come together in love and concern to act. God can do anything, and so he chooses to wait. He doesn't wait for me and he doesn't wait for you; he waits for *us* to unite in love and go forward in the confidence that God is our deliverer. God does not wait for the lone man to come in and exact vengeance so that the town is saved.

"Be devoted to one another in brotherly love. Honor one another above yourselves" (Romans 12:10). In this story, as with many stories throughout the history of humanity, these friends had to band together. Daniel and his friends were not at war, but their lives were in danger. They drew together to stay alive, but they also drew together to glorify their God.

They each prayed for the other. They went to seek out God and ask him not only for themselves but more importantly for the community they loved. They drew strength from each other and drew confidence in knowing they were not going to God alone; they had the comfort of knowing there was a community of people asking God for the same thing and a community of God concerned about them, and they were concerned about the community. They loved each other and banded together to try to save each other as well as the other wise men in the kingdom.

That is how God created us. That is how he wants us to be, in community with one another. I have to admit I still love the lone hero image. Whether it is John Wayne or Bruce Willis, I love the guy who is "that guy." But as much as I want to be "that guy" and save the day, God wants us to rely on each other; he wants for communities to solve the problems that come before them. God equips us to be part of one body.

Working independently, we can accomplish many nifty things. As part of the body I have seen the church "rub its belly and pat its head" many times. While it is impressive, it does nothing to further the kingdom of God. But when the whole body works together neighborhoods can change, lives can be transformed, wounds can heal, and life can begin again. That can take place only through community.

Heroes are wonderful; they're needed in our world. They are the stuff of myth and legend. But real things are accomplished by community, not by heroes. Lives are changed and restored through the community, but not just any community. I am part of many different types of communities. Most recently in my life I have become a part of the social networking community. I can't say I know how exactly it works, but I get notes from people I haven't seen in twenty years. I don't know how they found me or how they contacted me, but I've been very grateful they have. While this community is fun and it is great seeing and hearing from people far away, it doesn't change my life.

I've been part of the fantasy football community. We have a great time draft day and all season long, ribbing each other and trying to make the best trades possible. It makes the season fun and keeps things interesting when you live in a state with the record-setting Lions, the first NFL team in history to lose every game in the sixteen-week season.

As interesting as fantasy can be, it doesn't affect my life in tangible ways. The community that affects change in our lives must be rooted in something deeper than common interests or geography. A community must be rooted in something that can make change; it must be rooted in God.

While things seem to change all the time in our society, only God can really affect change and make our lives something greater and better than we can achieve on our own. Any community rooted in anything except God may produce images of change, even of confidence and acceptance, but the change will be fleeting at best.

The change people bring is mortal and finite. Alexander the Great changed the world, but it didn't affect me in any way. Twelve men and seven women went out in community to share the good news they had been given. My life has been irrevocably changed and will never resemble the life I had before. Their message not only changed me but also the entire world.

One person can do amazing things, but a community of God can transform the world.

CHAPTER 9

The Center

Sometimes I give myself the creeps,
sometimes my mind plays tricks on me.
It all keeps adding up, I think I'm cracking up
—Billy Joe Armstrong

In the year the Republican Party died, the Word of the Lord came to me and said "Get thee on a flying chariot and head south to where the clouds depart and the sun doth shine. While in that great and terrible land, take up thy pen and write. For I am the Lord your God and I am as sick of clouds and cold as the next guy, so go, and I will be with thee."

"You mean we're going to Disney World, Lord?" I asked.

"No, I don't like lines! But we'll play a little golf and lay on the beach," he said. "I need a tan."

May the Word of the Lord be done! I proclaimed; may the Word of the Lord endure forever. Let the Lord be praised! We're going to Florida—God is good. So in humble obedience to the Lord I left home, friends, and the land of my father with only fourteen clubs, a box of new Titleists, clean underwear, and two Bic ballpoints—black, of course.

My journey did not begin well. I inadvertently sat next to a feminism disciple on the plane and was intrigued enough to browse through a new best seller (for me this in itself is a sign of the end times) she had in her carry-on along with *Cosmo, Glamour, Self, Shape,* and a new-age meditation guide on how folks—through the proper use of hypnotic trance—can channel Suzanne Somers's thighs into their own legs.

The book on self-esteem talked about how we could gain worth from looking within. I gave the book only a cursory glance; it covered among other things meditation (self-hypnosis), self-discovery, and learning to communicate with your inner child. As I expected, the author was critical of most men, the church, religion (specifically anything as intolerant and suppressing of women as Christianity), and the God of the Bible. Of course, in some instances the author had some very good points. But in others she was very misinformed. But one page really grabbed my attention. She quoted Jesus—that's right, Jesus!—in small, innocuous, letters that nonetheless leapt off the page at me. I read the quote, read it again, and shook my head. I don't claim to have all of Scripture committed to memory, but I was quite sure Jesus never said what this author had quoted. I was absolutely sure Jesus wouldn't appreciate being misquoted in a way that made it appear he wholeheartedly endorsed transcendental self-discovery and new-age psychobabble.

Wait a minute, I thought. *There's a footnote at the end of the quote. Maybe it's a disclaimer, maybe an explanation.* I moved down the page and discovered a heartwarming explanation. This quote was taken from the Gnostic Gospels; written centuries after the life of Christ; they revealed a Jesus who presented himself as a compassionate teacher rather than the exclusive Son of God (how arrogant that would be). This Jesus of the Gnostic Gospels was more politically correct, more inclusive and accepting of all people (particularly women), and all behavior. He wasn't narrow-minded and judgmental, and best of all he didn't claim any authority or lordship over your life, my life, and, most of all, the author's life.

Again I shook my head. I realized the author had made some basic assumptions that seriously differed from my own, namely, that the Jesus of Matthew, Mark, Luke, and John was not a desirable Jesus and could therefore be discounted, even reinvented more to her liking (but that would be arrogant and judgmental). What the heck, I'll be arrogant and judgmental anyway—she was wrong.

I believe her basic assumptions were wrong, so even though her arguments flowed well and appeared to be validated by the words of Jesus, they were built on a false premise, a false statement. She didn't understand or like the Jesus she was aware of, and so she changed him (with a little help from the Gnostics) into someone a little more user-friendly. In essence she did what most of us do with Christ: we reinvent him to fit into our thoughts, ideas, and lifestyles.

This is what the following pages are somewhat about—the sin of recreating God into our image and how that affects the community in which we live. Of course we see this done in our mainstream culture. God is either recreated or denied. In fact, sometimes the church recreates God so the world won't deny the church, and we pat ourselves on the back.

It's Alive! It's Alive! *Ha ha ha ha ha*

The result of recreating God is that he judges a society by giving people over to their desires (Romans 1:18-32). The church sits back, scratches its head, and wonders why the world can continue to sin so blatantly and approve of those who do.

Christians who try to raise their voices of conscience meet with frustration because any argument invoking God, the authority of Scripture, or any other absolute is met with a set of basic assumptions that deny God ever existed, rendering such arguments meaningless. It's easy to condemn the world for its recreations of God and judge it for embracing a misinformed, self-serving set of assumptions. However, it seems to me that those of us in the church are often guilty of the same sin in a more subtle way.

One area this is most clearly seen in is the way we attempt to "be" the church. We too, I believe, tend to recreate God in our own image and recreate his church into an impotent imitation of the original. Obviously this is never our intent, but sadly it's the result. The church is no longer the Church. There, I've said it. The church as we know it is a political and social religious institution whose basic assumptions have been more shaped by the dominant values of our society (as our own desires) than by the dominant values of Scripture and the God revealed in Scripture. The church that once existed as a resident alien in a hostile and deceptive culture has now become an organization that affirms the pagan-dominant values of the culture in which we live. In our continuing grand attempts to "do" church we have lost the ability (and possibly the will) to "be" the church.

Just a point or two of the evidence that the church values society's values more than God's: the Catholic Church to a large extent affirms and embraces evolution. American Baptist churches openly accept pastors who are practicing homosexuals. Various branches of the Reformed Protestant faith still oppress and unfairly discriminate against women because they are women. Churches of every denomination ignore, hide, and sweep under the rug the sexual sins of their leaders.

Are You Really There?

I recently spent an afternoon with a church member (church leader, actually) about his own church experience and involvement. He is not only a church member; he is, by my account, a true Christian who loves the Lord. He's been involved in church leadership for years as a deacon and an elder, and he's served on several boards and committees in an attempt to lead and serve the body of Christ.

He and I talked for a couple of hours about joys, frustrations, God's will, more frustrations, and his church leadership experiences. I finally asked, "Alright, who are you really the church with?" He locked eyes with mine but didn't speak. I could sense his mind was processing the question, so I continued, "Who are you intimate with? Who can you pray honestly with? Who are you being discipled with on a regular basis? Who do you confess sin with and struggle with the realities of temptation in your life? Who challenges you? Who really loves you? Who can you be real and vulnerable with?"

My friend spoke after a thoughtful pause. "No one," he said. "I've been on boards, councils, committees in my church for years, but I'm not really 'the church' with anyone. I can honestly say I don't have a real, close friend within my church I can talk with like we've talked today."

He said it sadly. During the two hours we talked I sensed his passion, his concern, his "righteous" indignation, but then he was just sad. Our time together was done. We went back to his office and prayed before I left. We prayed for each other, for God to have free reign in our lives, and for the church—for ourselves—to be the church once again.

"Do you feel sufficiently busied by your church?" I asked a young mother who was very involved in her congregation. It seemed like I'd asked the question a hundred times the last month. "Oh, yes" came her enthusiastic reply. "We've got worship on Sunday morning along with Sunday school for the kids. Although we usually don't make Sunday nights, our oldest is in youth group and choir. I sing in the choir myself as well as attend women's Bible study. My husband serves on the facilities planning committee, and he used to be an elder, and we're both working on vacation bible school for the summer."

"Wow, that must keep you hopping," I said.

"Yes, it does," she smiled, "and that's just my church involvement."

"Tell me," I asked, "do you feel sufficiently challenged spiritually by your church?" I waited patiently for the predictable response. Rarely did I have to explain my question. Everyone knew what I meant, and everyone gave me the same reply. It began differently with each person but usually ended with something like "Church keeps me very busy."

As with my friend, there was a thoughtful pause. Then a sad realization surfaced. "No, not really. Amidst all the busyness of church activity for me and my family I still experience a spiritual void, a vacuum that all my busyness and activity doesn't quite fill."

What's wrong with this picture?

A Hunger for Flight

George Verwer in *Hunger for Reality* says most of us realize we live our Christian lives as "spiritual schizophrenics" who participate in church activity but never experience the transforming touch of Christ in our lives.

The Danish existentialist Søren Kierkegaard described most Christians as living like "practical atheists." We play brilliantly with Christianity and "Christian" activity. We enjoy its beauty in a detached manner and participate in church functions and worship, but all too seldom do we become passionately involved with Christ.

Kierkegaard tells the story of a make-believe land in which only ducks lived. One Sunday morning the ducks got up, brushed their feathers, and waddled to church. After waddling down the aisles and into their pews, they squatted. The duck minister waddled in and took his place behind the pulpit. He opened the duck bible to the place where it spoke of God's great gift to ducks, wings.

"With wings," said the duck preacher, "we ducks can fly. We can mount up like eagles and soar into the heavens. We can escape the confinement of pens and fences. We can know the utopia of complete freedom. We must give thanks to God for so great a gift as wings."

The duck congregation shouted "Amen!" and all waddled home.

Most of us, like the ducks, nod our heads and say "Amen!" but walk through life without committing ourselves heart, mind, and soul to the God who gave us wings, and consequently we never use the gift God has given. In the midst of church activity and busyness we still waddle.

Why is it so many people can invest in church programs, services, committees, and leadership yet still come up dry and thirsty? We are a lot like the golfer who was wildly celebrating his hole in one when it was pointed out to him that he had gotten it in the wrong hole. He had hit what he'd aimed for, but it was the wrong target.

The Bull's-eye

What are we aiming for? What is the center in the life and work of the church? If I were to draw a target of circles to illustrate five components of "success" in being the church, it would be like this: on the outside of the circle is our church's structure and strategy; the next ring toward the center contains our values, the next ring has our mission statement, and that's followed by the ring that includes our authentic leaders. At this point we are one small step from the center, God.

Notice that on the outer edge of the target is structure and strategy, which has to do with what we do and how we do it. This circle deals with programs (education, outreach, youth, evangelism, and music), facilities, styles, schedules, how we "do" worship and administer the church. It has to do with how we govern ourselves, make decisions, budget funds, and organize our body to meet its needs. This is where we act, where we attempt to "do" the work of Christ.

As we move toward the center, the next circle in our target, values. In theory our structure and strategy are dictated by the values we hold most high. It's in this circle that a church clarifies upon which mountains it is willing to die. For example, if a church values being flexible and offering choices based on an attitude of openness and acceptance, this will determine a lot about structure and strategy. A value that holds corporate worship as a priority for the church will dictate an appropriate structure and strategy.

As before, values flow naturally from the next ring toward the center—in this case a determined mission statement, one that communicates why the church exists. Inherent in such a mission statement is a definition of what we believe the church to be. Structure and strategy can then be evaluated in light of whether they fulfill the mission statement and affirm its values.

As we look at the target, we realize that no philosophy, value, structure, or strategy can truly be effective apart from the existence and continual emergence of authentic leaders. We also must realize that such leaders emerge not from the outer circles but from the inner circle, the bull's-eye—God. In the context of the Christian church, authentic leadership refers to the leaders who live in the middle of the circle. These leaders have experienced a sense of call and a commitment to obedience that comes from being in the presence of and in dialogue with God.

Authentic leaders are gifted and godly women and men who have come out of the center saying, "God, do something with me or let me die." Authentic leaders share a passion for obedience along with the qualities of vulnerability, transparency, and humility.

These leaders are directed by the Spirit of God as they seek him in the center, yet they are far from the sin of presumption, the attitude of "I have all the answers—I know the mind of God." Authentic leaders have gained a sense of call that God has initiated, but they do not act in a vacuum; it is only in the midst of community that they have a purpose and a role. It is only in an insula that these authentic people can be leaders.

God is always the initiator. Men and women who live in the center circle experience God. They confess sin, humble themselves before God, and set their minds to gain understanding from the Lord. In the center is where God speaks, where Scripture speaks. It's here that God's Spirit begins to transform our minds and conforms us to the image of Christ. It's here that we see God as he really is.

The Initiator

In Isaiah 6:1-13, God calls Isaiah. It's a center-of-the-circle experience. Isaiah says, "Woe to me." When we move into the center circle we get an awesome glimpse of God. He overwhelms us. We see him as he is, no longer as we want to see him. When I see God as he is, I tend to see myself as I really am. Like Isaiah (verse 5), my only response is "woe to me." I see my sin. This isn't pleasant, but it is necessary.

In my confession, God initiates forgiveness. He always initiates. He takes away my sin and my guilt and issues a call: "Who can I send? Who will go for me?" It is not about the individual. Once God has approached a person, it is not about that person anymore. God is calling authentic people to go out to the community, to step up, beyond themselves, into the world. Authentic leaders respond like Isaiah: "Here am I, Lord. Send me." It is precisely this experience that we long for when people declare voids in their church experience and pursuits. It is the lack of an encounter with God that they are describing. It is this experience for which we hunger.

Why do we miss it? I believe the modern-day church lives on the outside circle, obsessed with structure and strategy, programs, schedules, facilities, and agendas, while the inner circle becomes a vacuum. We mistakenly function as if people move from the outside in, and so we think if we get people involved in programs, classes, leadership, involvement, etc., they will move toward the inner circle.

Upside Down, Inside Out

In reality, movement goes from the inside out, so in the midst of the busyness of church we rarely experience the center, we rarely experience God. We tend to stay on the outside circles because it's safer, looks better, and is well organized and controlled.

The irony is that in the midst of attractive structure and strategy most churches are revolving doors for church members and God seekers. People come in, look around, and wander out. It's very possible to live on the outside of the circle with apparently great structure and strategy, but if action doesn't come from the inside circle, if it's not God's vision he's communicating while providing authentic leaders, the structure and strategy will fail. It may look good and boost attendance, involvement, and even offerings, but if it's not God's vision, it's temporary and bound to fail.

On the other hand, if intimacy with God in the center produces God's vision that is incorporated in the structure and strategy ring, then success is guaranteed because it's God's vision. Success in God's eye may not be what we envision; by our standards the prophet Isaiah was a miserable failure with a lousy strategy because when he preached, attendance dwindled. Yet this was God's vision (Isaiah 6:1-13).

Success meant obedience, which began in the center circle. Sometimes attendance didn't just dwindle. When the prophet Jeremiah spoke, the people wanted to kill him, and he was driven into the hills for fear of his life. Jeremiah spoke the Word of God so well not only did he lose his congregation, they wanted to kill him. But in God's eyes Jeremiah was a tremendous success.

Most churches and religious organizations will go only into the third circle. They develop philosophies of ministry and then stop there, assuming that's the center, so their philosophies may often be based on assumptions not directly from God but from the periphery.

I know from experience and Scripture that my ways and God's are not necessarily the same. In fact, in my life my ways are initially the exact opposite ways of God. The perplexing situation in the church is that quite often the unspiritual set the agenda for the spiritual.

We develop philosophies of ministry, values, and structures out of our own ignorance. We call upon the culture around us to help shape the directions we think we are to go. We call these values and structures experience and wisdom. We tend to produce grand plans and strategize for the next twenty years, which reflect an ever broadening outer circle while taking us farther from the inner circle. In these cases involvement may increase, but intimate experience with God will not.

People eventually become disillusioned, realizing that at best their church involvement is an empty charade. People slowly leave in search of other churches that can "meet their needs" or give up the search altogether. In response, the church seeks new, cutting-edge structures, strategies and programs to draw people back in. In reality these are gimmicks, desperate attempts to hold onto people who have never truly experienced intimacy with Christ and transformation by his Spirit.

Market-Driven Spirituality

We market the gospel of Christ to a consumerist society in hopes (and usually with noble motives) of drawing men and women into the church and thus to Christ. In this scenario the world represents the customer and the church becomes the salesman, offering a display case of programs, options, and entertainment from which consumers can pick and choose. Such a church becomes an accommodating church so intent on running errands for the world that it gives the world less and less in which to disbelieve. Slowly the church becomes a place where God really does not matter as we go about building bigger and better congregations that confirm people's self-esteem, enable people to adjust to their anxieties brought on by their materialism, and make Christ a worthy subject of poetic reflection.

At every turn the church must ask itself if its actions and implementations really make any difference in our lives together. Are we supplanting the truth that in Jesus Christ God is working in the world to reconcile people to himself? Are we truly becoming a community of God?

We become accommodating when we assume the real goal and ministry of the church is about "helping people" and making each other feel good. The trouble is we assume we know what helping people looks like, but if our ideas come more from the society we live in and popular culture than from a true center of the circle experience directed by God's Word, we're probably mistaken.

Most professing Christians, oftentimes especially leadership, live like practical atheists because they think the church survives, grows, and is sustained by the services it provides or the amount of fellowship and good feeling in the congregation. There's nothing wrong with services or good feelings; what is wrong is when they become ends in themselves. When this happens, the church and ministry cannot avoid sentimentality. That is the attitude of being always ready to understand but not to judge. This corrupts ministry and in fact makes real ministry impossible.

The bottom line is that we are not called to help people by pacifying them in the lukewarm nature of our society to make them feel good. We are called to follow Jesus; there's joy in following Christ. But I find it's possible that rather than meeting all my hopes and dreams for success and happiness in this life, he transforms my mind to the point that my hopes and dreams truly become his.

Perhaps when I follow Christ I begin to realize I am so at odds with the world around me I may actually lose my family, job, security, happiness, affluent lifestyle, status, and comfort. I may find the call of Christ means taking up a cross and following him. I may find the world will hate me because it hated him. I may find I am called to be radically changed, to be so transformed by the Spirit of God that I lay down my life as a living sacrifice and no longer conform to the image of this world. Perhaps following Christ has more to do with his changing my needs, wants, and desires than in his fulfilling them. Maybe he gives me what my heart desires only when my heart desires his things.

Compatibility Issues

It's time to realize the dominant values of our culture and society are not God-ordained. It's time to acknowledge that Western American, middle-class Christianity may not be compatible with the Christianity of Scripture. It's time to recognize that no longer do we live in a Christian society, if we ever did, but must exist as resident aliens opposed to an anti-"God of the Bible" culture.

Romans 12:1-2 urges us to give ourselves to God as living sacrifices. This is true worship—not conforming to the image of this world, not buying into the dominant values of secular society, but being transformed by renewing our minds. We are to be changed by the Holy Spirit as we encounter God in the center and from there offer him our heart, mind, soul, and body. Then and only then will we truly be able to discern and understand God's will and vision for our lives individually and corporately as his church.

I realize this has been mainly about the church, but it applies as strongly to our lives outside the institutional church as well. The institutional church is in the state it's in because of the individuals who make up the church. We are the ones who are agenda-driven, busy twenty-four hours a day, seven days a week, fifty weeks a year. The other two weeks we're off at some sunny or wintery resort, forgetting our lives and the world we have to go back to. We are more concerned about how we look than how we truly are. We are concerned if we are doing enough to get ahead. We are trying everything we can, including stepping on others to get what we deserve. Yet this is the exact mentality that keeps us from being community with others, from being an insula and caring for others as Christ calls us to.

We have stopped caring for those around us and have begun to believe caring about ourselves is our highest priority. If parents let kids stay in the home past age twenty, society looks at them in disgust. If we take aging parents home instead of settling them into a care facility, we are asked if that is really in our best interests and those of the aging parents. If we take in someone who doesn't have a home, the culture at large is shocked that we would endanger ourselves by doing so: "What about privacy? How can you have any privacy with another person there?" We have taken God's values and thrown them out with the bathwater. We have found society's values nice and soft and cushy and have adopted those, but just to be safe we declare them to be "God-ordained." We aren't rejecting God; God changed when Jesus came to town. Now we don't have to take care of those God brings into our lives; we have agencies for that. And really, what they need is money, so I'll just write a check, and that'll cover me.

When You Assume

Too often people have brought in the dominant values of our society without seriously taking the examples of Scripture into account. In fact, such societal values have become the basic assumptions through which the church interprets Scripture and the foundation on which we have sought to be the body of Christ. Let me share what I believe to be a few of these dominant values.

Individualism is noble. Our nation was built on rugged individualism as conservative pundits so enthusiastically remind us. The message of our culture is that to be successful and strong means making it on our own. We need help from no one, including God, so nobody should depend on help from us. Since we are to survive and succeed on our own, we become isolated from those around us unless they are able to further our agendas. We lose intimacy, and dependence on others is interpreted as weakness.

We seek in our society not only to be financially independent but to be independently wealthy not so much to keep from being a burden to others but because we are proud, independent people who never want to be subject to another's provision, even God's.

Ironically, the church is always described as an intimate community not only socially but also emotionally, physically, materially, and spiritually. Spiritual independence usually means spiritual paralysis. To be independent in any area usually means an ineffective faith because faith is demonstrated by works, and we desperately need one another in order to be spurred on to good works (James 2, Hebrews 10). However, what we call the church is too often a gathering of strangers who see the church as another helping institution to further gratify their individual desires.

In *Resident Aliens,* Stanley Hauerwas and William H. Willimon state: "The church is often a conspiracy of cordiality" in which we learn to pacify one another rather than disciple believers and confront sin. "We say we do it out of 'love'. Usually we do it as a means of keeping everyone as distant from everyone else as possible" (p. 138).

Infringement

Of course, one of the most distasteful and worldly excuses for Christianity is legalism, which imposes man-made chains on people Christ intended to live freely. There is often a fine line between Christian liberty and personal pursuit. For example, in America I have the right to pursue my own happiness, which usually means I can choose any behavior or lifestyle I want as long as it doesn't infringe on anyone else's right or ability to do the same. I have the right to live how I want without you telling me what is "right or wrong."

No individual can impose values and behavior on another; we get to choose for ourselves. This sounds well and good at first glance; after all, the Bible itself says we are not to judge, right? It's appropriate to find what works for me and pursue it. In essence this is a sophisticated enactment of the original sin—pride. It's one way our society and too often the Christian church is constantly reshaping God into their own images. One only has to watch a talk show to hear a host or an enlightened audience member argue with a spokesperson of the religious right about what type of God God is; most of the time God becomes whoever or whatever we want him to be. God is accepting, tolerant, and nonjudgmental and would never infringe on someone's personal rights and freedoms. But this is our view of who we want God to be, not God's view of who he truly is. The spiritual person judges all things (1 Corinthians 2:15, 5:12), and spiritual leaders are entrusted to judge the church with great humility. It's very important for the church to not only argue that God exists but to incarnate what kind of God he truly is.

When it was reported that President Bill Clinton's Baptist faith was so personal that he didn't even talk about it with his Methodist wife, we applauded the implied nobility of someone unwilling to impose spiritual values or convictions on another person—even a spouse. But what type of faith-filled world do we live in where we cannot share our faith with the person closer to us than anyone else? If we can't share our faith with that person, we can't share our faith at all, leaving Jesus' greatest command completely unfulfilled.

Wealth and consumerism are good. While political parties can't agree on whether God is Democrat or Republican, most Americans pretty much agree he's a capitalist. In America, I have a "God-given" right to pursue the American dream: to be wealthy and independent.

Most modern presidential campaigns reinforce how strongly this value is cherished along with personal freedom. We are a consuming society, a society that wants our hearts' desires, and the Bible says God wants to give us our hearts' desires, so wanting things is ordained by God. How can we help the poor of this world if we are poor ourselves? We won't be able to do anything or help anyone if we are struggling every day just to put food on the table. Having things is okay as long as those things don't own you.

But when was the last time you saw someone with a brand-new, huge, all-terrain vehicle who was willing to sell it and give the almost $100,000 to a poor family so they could buy a house or simply buy food? It doesn't happen that often. Since I don't know all of those who own vehicles that cost more than a house, I don't want to say God hasn't done something like that. But even though I live in a community with a plethora of churches and a boatload of expensive cars, I have never seen or heard of anybody giving up a prize possession to care for someone else.

A church near me just finished an addition that cost more than fifteen million. While the building is beautiful and awe-inspiring, how many single mothers who don't have homes could we have given homes to with that money? How many cars could we have given to people who can't work because they don't have reliable transportation? How many kids going hungry could we have fed? But the building is very beautiful.

We have taken the biblical phrase "see the lilies of the field . . . how much more does God care about you?" (Matthew 6:28) as a mandate to get as much as we can. We no longer strive to be content with where we are; we now long to have enough so we never have to settle for simply being content.

Silence and inaction are the enemy

I am here to be entertained, and if I ever find myself bored and quiet, I must find something to stimulate me. This could be found in the toys I buy, the games I play, the movies I watch, the shopping I do, the parties I attend, and of course the church activities I busy myself with.

Ironically, my entire culture lives in what I call "entertainment escape." Probably much of what is done in churches with so-called contemporary or modern worship services is nothing more than a sacrifice brought to the altar of entertainment. Skits, drums, videos, and dance are often less expressions of faith and worship than attempts to hold the audience's attention for an hour on Sunday. This addiction to entertainment is a primary distraction in our pursuit of the center of the circle; not a lot of entertainment happens there. Today's television images can go as quickly as four images or shots per second, but not in the center. And rarely do people applaud and flick their lighters.

Blipverts Abound

It's no wonder the church lives on the outside of the circle; there's a lot more stimulation there. I think one of the greatest TV shows was a quirky, futurist show that came out in the 1980s called *Max Headroom.*

The plot of the first episode, the show in which Max is "born," involves blipverts, advertisements that squeezed about a hundred commercials into one thirty-second spot. The dilemma comes when these ads start to blow people up. When couch potatoes watch them, their lethargic lifestyle can't handle the massive stimulation and they blow up, hence the mystery that must be solved.

We are quickly approaching blipverts in today's society. While I don't believe anyone will blow up from them, I do believe when people simply quote life-changing passages, we tune out and turn off because they didn't captivate us within the first three seconds. Web designers will tell you that you have three to five seconds to capture viewers' attention or they'll go to another site. People bang on computer keyboards and hit monitors when uploads take more than eight seconds. We are a society that wants to be entertained not in five seconds but *now*.

When the church lives on the outside of the circle, busily creating structures and developing strategies void of the inner-circle experience, we usually end up validating the values of the world, and rarely does anyone point out the incongruities.

Trust the Force, Luke

The trouble with living on the outer circles is that if we look at the world, we see a culture rapidly falling apart and screaming for something solid to hold on to. The world tries to find it with inner peace and in tapping into the universal force all around us, but in truth the only living force we need to tap into is God. All the other things we busy ourselves with are just that: busyness. When the ride stops even for just a short while, we begin to feel emptiness and grab the first thing—anything—that will ease the lonely screams inside. The church has not helped society by living on the outer circle; we have simply reinforced the notion that this is all there is.

There is nothing deeper; there is no center. This is how a man who wrote a book became the leader of a religious movement that is growing rapidly in society today. Scientologists proclaim they have the secret and that part of it is inner peace, inner silence. The society around us wants the peace of God so much that when the church refuses to lead them to God they will grab hold of anything that looks good and claim it's the hand of God when actually it's a golden calf. In the absence of Moses' true leadership, his people went back to what they knew—comfortable rituals, not the God of peace and joy.

We need inclusiveness to truly be godly. I've had the privilege of taking part in quite a few conferences and Christian conventions. Usually they have been youth oriented, and nothing really shocking comes from the front. Occasionally I have been at a meeting at which the Bible has been reinterpreted to be inclusive and to not offend people. This doesn't sound so bad. What's wrong with making people feel included in Bible discussions? Most of the time I would agree with that assessment, but when the leader prays to "Mother" God or recites the Lord's Prayer "Praying as Jesus taught us, Our creator which art in heaven . . ." Mother? Creator? These are not the words of the Bible, the words God revealed to us. Just because men throughout history have been scumbag jerks does not give anyone the right to say to God, "You can't be seen as a loving father because my father was bad." They had bad male role models in their lives and so they replaced Father with Creator, but it's all the same thing, right? It's not.

Jesus was talking about a personal relationship with the Lord of all. The Lord's Prayer begins with Father. The Aramaic word is *Abba,* which means father but can also just as easily be translated as daddy or papa. Jesus has us become intimately involved with God the Father, the one from whom we come, the one who gave us life, the one to whom we go with our needs and concerns. "Father" is a very intimate word in a familial community such as the Jewish community Jesus came from.

You did not call people family in an arbitrary way. Growing up, I had several moms in the neighborhood. If you had a son around my age and weren't the Wicked Witch of the West, you became Mom, but that was my culture. Jesus was stepping outside of his culture in teaching his disciples to address God in such an intimate way. Out of reverence for God the Hebrews did not say the name of God; they did not even spell it for fear that in writing it someone might accidently say it. We call God Yahweh, but in truth that's just our best guess. You do not for the sake of inclusiveness change God the Father to God the Mother. You do not take the intimate relationship between a father and his son or daughter and change it to a cold, meaningless relationship between the created and the creator. Inclusivity does not mean we change God's word.

If you had a bad father, I am truly sorry, but know that you actually had a bad dad. Your Father was always looking out for you and watching carefully. Jesus tells his disciples in Matthew 23:9, "And do not call anyone on earth 'father,' for you have one Father, and he is in heaven." The relationship with God is so personal and intimate that God doesn't even want us to refer to our biological dad as father. We have only one Father, and he is in heaven. God takes his role as our Father very personally. How dare we change who he is so we don't offend someone? How dare we tell God he cannot be who he is so some might not get mad?

Our Values vs. God's Values

Faith is not just personal, and individualism is not a biblical ideal; it's more often pride disguised. Christianity is not self-serving; perhaps a follower of Christ has no personal rights or freedoms. Maybe a living sacrifice is dead to self and selfish pursuits. Maybe someone who has taken up a cross to follow Christ no longer pursues the American dream. It could even be that wealth and possessions are not so much God's blessing as they are God's curse on a body of cultural Christians who would really rather have God serve them than serve God.

In Luke chapter 8, Jesus tells a parable of a farmer who planted seeds. Some of the seeds, the Word of God, fell on a path and were snatched by birds before any plants—faith—sprouted. Some seeds fell on rocks, and plants sprang up quickly, but when the sun came out, they died because they had no roots. Some seeds fell among thorns. They produced plants, but the plants were eventually choked by the thorns. Jesus describes the thorns as riches, possessions, or pleasures and worries of this life. Isn't that amazing? Jesus tells us very plainly that the very things we pursue in our society, the very things our culture holds up as worthy of gain are what chokes our faith.

Most of our worries are brought on by our wealth or lack thereof, affluence, and materialism. We worry about how we will ever make ends meet even though we're in the top 4 percent of the world's wealthiest. We have chosen to live in debt and pursue things diametrically opposed to the growth of our faith and thus bring upon ourselves worries, all the while deceiving ourselves into believing we are being faithful to God all along. There is probably no more deadly adversary to the gospel and its church than wealth. We seek security in wealth. We are all like Ananias and Sapphira in Acts 5. We say with our lips, "Yes God, we've given you everything," but he knows our hearts are self-serving, self-preserving. It's a good thing he doesn't deal with us the way he did with them.

All anyone has to do is read the Sermon on the Mount to realize God's basic assumptions are a lot different from our own. Our society's dominant values are turned 180 degrees from those of Scripture. When we are told to no longer be conformed to the image of this world, it means more than just being moral people or nice people. It means being so radically committed to the faith we profess and the God who loves us that we reject the materialism, consumerism, and individualism of our society. We are called to reject not only immorality but also greed, pride, power, self-service, self-promotion, and self-deceit. We reject the pursuit of personal pleasure, comfort, and happiness while embracing Christ's invitation to be transformed. As we begin to gravitate toward the inner circle individually and corporately, we are conformed by the Spirit of God into the image of Jesus. Unless that happens, the church will die, not from crucifixion but from the soul's sheer boredom.

The Holy Spirit of God alone is the powerful, moving, dynamic force in the church. He alone grows the church; he alone convicts humanity of its sins; he alone softens hearts and draws people to Christ. I can really do nothing for God he can't do apart from me; I'm merely a privileged participant in the body of Christ as God moves through his people.

The New Testament describes a body empowered by the Holy Spirit. This Spirit was active in the lives of those who made up the church. He was more than a concept or theory affirmed in our creeds. The Holy Spirit was demonstrative. Yes, people were healed and the church grew; Peter preached, and three thousand believers were added to the church. Why? Because Peter was a great communicator and TV evangelist? No. His sermon wasn't that dynamic or poetic; it really wasn't very insightful, nor was it peppered with pithy quotes or stirring illustrations. It was God. It was the Holy Spirit. God moved and drew men and women through repentance to himself. God did it; Peter was just the vessel through which God spoke. If you look back to when God first called Israel to be a nation, its sins caused three thousand Israelites to die (Exodus 32:28). Bringing three thousand back to the kingdom was, I believe, God healing his children through Christ. Bringing them back was God bringing back to his covenant those who would be his children; it was a beginning movement in the church toward the center. And if you believe that three thousand being killed in Exodus and the same number being added at Pentecost is a coincidence, then you and I don't serve the same God.

Experiencing God, God's Way

As I read Scripture, I realize that such a real experience of the Holy Spirit in my life is little more than a fairy tale. I hunger for such a reality, but in all honesty I do not know it either in my personal life or in my church. I am not speaking of a pursuit of signs and wonders as characterized by charismatic movements but rather a pursuit of the Spirit who wants to empower men and women, whether through the miraculous or through the grind of daily obedience, to be witnesses and ministers, the body of Christ.

Signs and wonders have their places in the historical, biblical context and in the world today. God has always drawn people to him by the miraculous, but what is more miraculous than seeing God himself? In this world people are healed every day, people are being raised from the dead, ten days dead, but none of that compares to the majesty of being face-to-face with the Father of all creation; none of that compares to the glory that is God.

Perhaps the fundamental question then is not what structure and strategy do I adopt or what program can I offer to best help people, but how can I get in touch with the Holy Spirit? How can I find the center?

I do not presume to place the Spirit of God in a box. He can move and do what he wills. However, I find scripture principles to be true. The Spirit of God empowers those who wait, i.e., those who live in the middle of the circle (Isaiah 40). We mistakenly think God moves through our human efforts, and so we often adopt the strategies of the world as we develop outreach strategies, teaching techniques, and worship styles. The buzz phrase here is "cutting-edge ministry."

I was asked to write my reflections on what's new, cutting-edge, in ministry. I'm sure those who requested these thoughts expected an article detailing the new wave of creative, outer-circle programming that has impacted our culture for Christ. Perhaps the following will shed some light on what truly is cutting edge.

Picture this: The greatest Christian event in Michigan history with over 60,000 people packed in a stadium. Pizzas are parachuted in while the hottest Christian music groups team up for a rock, grunge, and metal tribute to the music of Keith Green. Nationally recognized speakers recreate the story of Nicodemus from John chapter 3 in the theatrical style of *Wayne's World*. Finally a band plays "Make My Life a Prayer to You" as tens of thousands respond to the altar call by flocking toward the giant overhead plasma screen. Perhaps we should break the crowd into dyads and triads to stimulate small-group discussion and motivate people to do service projects?

The cutting edge: it's where creativity and innovation meet pragmatism and results. Youth ministry by nature is cutting edge because young people and their culture are cutting edge, new, creative, and bizarre. Sometimes it's offensive and uncomfortable, and sometimes it's wonderfully artistic, energetic, insightful, and profound, but it's always changing.

So the tendency when thinking about the cutting edge of ministry is to ask What's new? What's different? How can I grab attention and relate a little better to the increasingly alien world and people of this generation? What's the gimmick?

Sorry—there's no gimmick. I can't give you a twelve-step plan, a three-point outline, or dynamic new program ideas that will magically produce a wonderful ministry and committed disciples of Jesus Christ. After all, that's the goal, isn't it, to somehow allow God to use me in reproducing committed disciples of Christ?

I have a very simple suggestion. If you want to be on the cutting edge of ministry as a professional (whatever that is) or a volunteer, become a committed disciple of Jesus Christ—that's it. It's that simple, and it's that difficult. Saying you'll become a disciple is easy, but becoming one will be the absolute, hardest thing you'll ever do living in modern American society.

Is Belief Discipleship?

Believing in Christ as Lord and Savior does not make you a disciple of Christ. You are saved as best we can know through that act. You can even call yourself a follower of Christ through the act of belief, but belief in Christ does not make you a disciple. Being a disciple of Christ means wanting to become exactly like Jesus. If every single area of your life is not subject to becoming more like Christ, you are not a disciple.

There is nothing wrong with being just a follower. As in Jesus' day, not that many people today are cut out to be disciples. We are all called to be priests in the kingdom of God, but we are not all called to be disciples.

In Hebrew the word was *talmidim*, meaning wise student. Those who do not qualify for this title could and still can be considered wise, but there is a life behavior as well as intellectual wisdom that comes with the title talmidim. It's greater than just passionate belief; it reflects a level of commitment we don't see too much anymore in our culture.

The church is called to live in a committed way in the light of that grace. This means maintaining a balance between attitude and action. In humility and dependence we continually see men and women through the eyes of Christ and seek to draw people into the kingdom of God.

Yes, the church is called to care. In some ways the church is a hospital for sick people, but it's a M.A.S.H unit near the front lines rather than a retirement home nestled in a peaceful countryside. When a church's purpose becomes maintaining itself and pacifying its members, it becomes very easy to tolerate the "small moves for small gains" mindset. When a church adopts its value system from popular culture, it loses the authority to deal head-on with true conviction. We look like we're working very hard, but truthfully we're inept at making a difference. Only as we consciously and sometimes forcibly keep our eyes fixed on Jesus do we perceive his mindset, perspective, and vision. Only then do we lay down our lives as sacrifices and pick up a sense of God's vision and call; only then can we truly begin to be a people called to form an insula. We will be a church that lives in the middle of the circle and acts from the center.

Center living is where we must strive to begin our journey because it's where God is. If we truly wish to be the bride of Christ, then we must know where the bridegroom is. If we do not pay attention to where the bridegroom is, we will miss him altogether, we will never meet him, we will cease to become the bride and just become a waiting visitor.

Fascinating, Mr. Spock

I believe the Holy Spirit alone is the creative, dynamic, driving force of the church. The Spirit brings about cutting-edge ministry. But the only way I get in touch with the Holy Spirit is by waiting. Ironic, isn't it? Those on the cutting edge of ministry will be those who take the time to do nothing.

I find it fascinating that at Christ's ascension he tells his followers to go to Jerusalem and do nothing. They are to wait. Wait? After a week and a half, when those waiting Christians least expected it, the Holy Spirit moved with demonstrative power and the church was born. They weren't just sitting in the upper room and waiting in secret when they returned to Jerusalem after Jesus' ascension. Luke 24:53 tells us the disciples left from Jesus and went back and were daily in the temple praising God. Acts 2, where the story picks up again, states that the disciples were in the "house." This is where our culture confuses our reading. The Jews called the temple the "house" because it was God's house. So Luke writes that they were at the house when the wind came. It does not mean, as we would think, that they were at the dwelling place of a disciple or even the upper room; they were in the temple, praising and worshiping God while they waited. Waiting is not necessarily a sedentary thing. There's often activity that happens while you wait for God. Even Jesus (Son of God, Messiah, Holy One, Bread of Life—you get the picture) spent forty days in the desert before he began his public ministry. Why? Sure he was tempted three times, but how long could that have taken? I was tempted three times before breakfast this morning. He waited. He struggled. He conversed with his father. Luke tells us that at the end of forty days he returned to Galilee "in the power of the Holy Spirit."

That's it: cutting-edge ministry involves those empowered by the Holy Spirit in the discipline of doing nothing, and it allows the Holy Spirit to do abundantly more than we can ask or think of. Cutting-edge ministry is done by those who desperately and actively seek the center.

1 Corinthians 1 and 2 say our wisdom is foolishness. Our strength is weakness, our creativity is boring, our clever arguments are unintelligible, our charisma is stoic, and much of what we busily do in the name of cutting-edge ministry is a waste of time. At worst it robs the cross of Christ of its power (1 Corinthians 1:17) because rather than

draw people to the unexplainable, holy, loving, sacrificial Christ of the cross, we draw people to ourselves by trying to make Jesus intellectually appealing and emotionally satisfying. The cross is foolishness to men and women whose belief systems and world views are more shaped by the big screen, the small screen, DVDs, *Cosmo,* and their "God is dead" experiences than by me and my cutting-edge ministry.

Do nothing—because nothing works. Call in sick tomorrow and, like Daniel (Daniel 9-10), humble yourself before God. Confess sin and set your mind to gain understanding from the Lord. (Daniel 10:12) Wait. Pray. Read. The weapons you must fight with are spiritual anyway (2 Corinthians 10:3-5), and the enemy you battle is an enemy you don't even see or understand (Ephesians 6:10-18). Sounds a little cutting edge, doesn't it? As you seek God and become a committed disciple of Jesus Christ by doing nothing but waiting, reading, and praying, the Holy Spirit will empower you to do ministry in ways you didn't think you could. God will even give you direction in how to lead the ministry you're involved with, and best of all it will be his vision for you, not mine or any other person's.

Let the Wait Begin

A while ago I heard a story. A game, much like Monopoly, has pieces to move, dice to roll, and squares to land on. The squares around the board represent qualities of a successful and growing church, including increased attendance and participation, spiritual growth of membership, discipleship programs, small-group Bible studies, attitudes of compassion and service, effective evangelism, a mission program, a dynamic Sunday school—you name it, it's on the board along with some things new players never heard of before or understood. A group was playing it, and a new player rolled the dice, anxious to get going and excited about the prospects of adding properties to his portfolio. When a seven came up, he began to move his piece.

"Hold it" said one of the other players. "Don't you know the rules?"

"I thought I did," the new player replied. "What am I doing wrong?"

"You can't move until the red bird comes and lands on your shoulder."

"What . . . the red bird? I don't see any red bird."

"Exactly" instructed the other player. "That's why you must wait."

To his dismay several hours passed of rolling the dice and moving nowhere. He waited for the red bird, beginning to doubt it even existed although he heard the other players talk about it. So one time, when his turn came, he rolled the dice again—an eight. He absentmindedly passed the dice to the next player but got them back. He realized there was a red bird perched on his left shoulder. He cautiously moved out eight spaces from square one. His heart raced. What property would he acquire? He landed on a square that instructed him to draw a card. He reached for it anticipating great things, maybe "Roll Again" or "Move to the Space of Your Choice." Instead, the cards read simply and coldly, "Go Back to Square One." He couldn't believe it. After all this waiting he was told to go back to the beginning?

When it was his turn again, he rolled the dice with enthusiasm. Twelve; he started to move but was stopped. To his horror he realized the red bird had left his shoulder sometime between his last roll and this one. So once again he waited. His turns came and went, and still he waited. Eventually the bird returned, and our player moved out from square one only to land on a square that instructed him to draw a card. He anticipated great things, but the card also read "Go Back to Square One."

This frustrating pattern continued until finally he could stand it no longer.

"I quit!" he screamed.

"Why?" asked another, more-experienced player. "You've been doing quite well."

"Quite well?" he asked with astonishment. "I've been playing this game all night and haven't got one property to show for my efforts."

"You misunderstand the game," the experienced player said light-heartedly. "You think the object is to get as far as you can around the board and accumulate properties. That isn't the goal at all. The object is to always go back to square one, where you can wait for the Holy Spirit."

"The Holy Spirit?" the man asked.

"Yes, the red bird. He's the game master. He'll take you to any square he wants you to go, but that's incidental. Your goal is to wait for him. Don't you understand if you were to gain a property without the red bird, you'd lose more than you gain? Go back to square one; that's where you always want to be."

Square one, the middle of the circle, the bull's-eye, the center—that's our goal, our pursuit, and believe it or not our end. So wait.

Waiting brings me to the point of humility and brokenness. It is here I lose my self-reliance and trust totally and completely in God, who is able to do immeasurably more than we can even imagine. The sacrifice that God seeks is not effort, talent, performance, or human abilities but a broken heart (Psalm 51:17). Everyone who was called by the Lord, empowered, and used was first brought to a point of self-emptying, humble dependence. Our God resists and opposes the proud but offers his grace to the humble (James 4:6-10). He demands submission to himself, confession of sin, and a purified heart. When we humble ourselves before the Lord, he will lift us up.

In the center circle I can dialogue with God through prayer and his Word. Too often we look for God's vision and will for our lives and the church in every place but the center. We strategize out of ignorance. We have church-growth consultants who give us a plethora of outer-circle ideas that have worked elsewhere, but the obvious question is worked at doing what? Usually the answer is they have worked at enlarging the vacuum rather than pulling people to the center of the circle and an encounter with Christ.

It's Always Greener

We look around at other churches and see what has been successful as if the church was a wavering economy that could be jump-started through a stimulus package. Sometimes we let people dictate God's leading for the church by asking the marketing question, "What do you want? You're the customer." So we decide we want a larger building and more excellent worship, so we hire professionals to give us better music, more-interesting education, better preaching, and a jazzier youth ministry. We develop opportunities for every age group, social class, and area of interest under the sun. It's a buyer's market, and the customer is king. However, the church is not customer-owned or driver-operated. It is owned by God, and it exists for his glory, not to satisfy our agendas. So Scripture is indeed the first blueprint to consult when it comes to shaping the church. I wonder how many church leaders confront Scripture from the humility of the center circle, asking the questions, What is the church? What does it look like? How does it function? The reason is that most people are much more interested in having a church than in being the church.

Prayer in the center circle is more listening than talking. Too often our prayers are monologues in which we pray for the sick, thank God for the weather, and ask his blessing on our self-centered pursuits. Prayer is a process. The problem is that most of us view it as the process by which my will becomes God's will (here's what I want God—now please do it). However, prayer is the process by which God's will becomes our will. It is an active process that happens in the quiet waiting in that center circle. Only here will God rearrange my desires to align with his own. Only here does the spirit transform my mind to conform to the mind of Christ. Only here do I present my body, mind, and soul as a living sacrifice, and only then do I begin to discern God's good and perfect will—those properties of church pursuits that make up the outer circle of structure and strategy. It's usually at this point that we become surprised at what God's vision for his church may be.

We demonstrate our openness to the Holy Spirit through continual obedience. Perhaps the most difficult area for obedience, individually and corporately, is in the area of finances. This is especially true for affluent, upper-middle-class, American Christians—you and me. When we speak of wealth and other worldly things, we do have to approach them from God's perspective. When we see through the eyes of God, which see farther than beyond our own block or city, we see globally. When I speak of the upper middle class, I'm not speaking of people who earn more than we do. I'm speaking of people who own two vehicles and three televisions and a home and a cottage, condo, or trailer somewhere else. Americans are consistently wealthier than other people in this world; even compared to those in developed countries Americans outshine in the area of possessions. We have more, seek more, and eat more than people anywhere else. The Lord is pretty clear in his attitude about wealth, but we conveniently rationalize away Scripture that says "sell your possessions and give to the poor" (Luke 12:33). Obviously, such a radical, ridiculous command couldn't be meant for me or my church, could it?

"Be faithful in the little things and you will be given greater things" (Luke 16:10). In the parable of the minas (Luke 19), Jesus says "to whoever has, more will be given." In the parable of the shrewd manager (Luke 16), Jesus says something to the effect that whoever can be trusted with very little can also be trusted with much. So if you have not been trustworthy in handling worldly wealth, who will trust you with real riches? In Christ's parable material wealth means just that—money. But the greater riches indeed seem to be spiritual, not only in heaven but here in this life. I don't think it's a stretch to paraphrase, "Be obedient with your money, and I can entrust you with my spirit." What then does obedience mean? Could it be a radical transformation that causes affluent people of God to reject the materialistic values of our culture and actually give away money and possessions rather than store them up in self-consuming silos? Is it possible that one of the highest challenges for a church, even a wealthy church, is to live in such a way as to enable its people to simplify their consumerist lifestyles and thereby free up the incredible wealth God has entrusted us with to further his kingdom by giving it away?

The principle is that if I'm not faithful with the material, God may not bless me with the spiritual. This cannot be overlooked, especially when I acknowledge I live in a spiritual reality. Peretti's novels may or may not be good theology, but they are a great reminder that the spiritual world is real. I do not wrestle against flesh and blood; my battle is in another realm (Ephesians 6:12). I don't have to be a tongue-wagging, hand-waving Pentecostal charismatic TV evangelist to understand this. We do not wage war as the world does because the war is spiritual, so I must allow God's spirit to have free movement in my life. Scripture teaches implicitly and explicitly that a lack of faithfulness in the material hinders the spiritual presence and movement in the nonmaterial.

We are rich. It doesn't always seem like it because we compare ourselves to those around us. We do this in every area of life, and it often can lead to either arrogant superiority or disabling self-pity. We Americans are in the top 4 percent of the world when it comes to wealth. The reason we struggle to make ends meet on a family income of $50,000 or more a year is that we've adopted the lifestyles of our society and live in constant debt in order to gratify our materialistic desires. Bluntly put, it's a sinful lifestyle. However, it's quite understandable since most of us have grown up in the society we live in and have been conditioned since birth that an affluent, consumerist lifestyle is not only perfectly normal but something to strive for. We don't know any better. If we go almost any other place in the world we begin to know better.

The Mall Principle

A contributing factor to our mindset and one of the subtle evils of our culture is what I call the mall principle. This principle operates in my life this way: I am perfectly content until I walk through a mall and see all the things I don't have. The more I see, the more I want. The more I want, the more I can't help but purchase what I want. Our society creates desires that are very difficult to keep from gratifying particularly when the means are readily available. We need to open our eyes and realize we don't act in isolation. With increased technology, our world is rapidly shrinking, and I can potentially impact any place or people I choose. When I bow to the mall principle I make a choice to not feed a child in Bolivia. Whether I realize it or not, I have made a choice. A center of the circle mindset might adopt the perspective that my worldly wealth is not really my own but is entrusted to me by God. I am in a sense his stockbroker. If I hoard or consume the material blessings he has given me, he cannot, will not entrust me with spiritual wealth. God may and will withhold his Holy Spirit because he knows I will do exactly the same with him that I do with my own money, hoard it or consume it. This is true corporately as well.

Faithfulness with resources means more than investing in an IRA with a 10-percent annual yield; it means more than propagating church programs, budgets, and building projects that are more self-serving and self-consumptive than we'd ever admit. Faithfulness means investing entrusted wealth in feeding the hungry, clothing the naked, and housing the homeless. This is part of the product and process of living in the middle of the circle.

The Gospel of Luke talks quite a bit about wealth. If I didn't know better I'd swear it was not only a matter of obedience but also of salvation. Didn't Jesus say we can love and serve God or we can love and serve money? It can't be both (Luke 16:13). Of course we would say we don't love money (after all, that's the root of all evil, isn't it?); we just have it. When Jesus tells the rich, young ruler (Luke 18) to sell his possessions and give the money to the poor, we somehow think it was an easier proposition for him than for us, or else we think that Jesus asked for such drastic action not because the ruler was rich but because his priorities were out of line. Of course, the very way the young ruler (or we) get our priorities in line may be by selling our possessions and giving the money to the poor.

What I have is not my own. In the eternal scheme of things I must give out my wealth, and in order to truly be the church I must live in some sort of community with others of the same mindset. Usually this begins with the difficult task of confession and repentance.

What else does Luke reveal about the mind of Christ concerning riches in this world? Naturally the best way to find out is to read the book, but let's highlight some passages:

> And he came down with them and stood on a level place, with a great crowd of his disciples and a great multitude of people from all Judea and Jerusalem and the seacoast of Tyre and Sidon, who came to hear him and to be healed of their diseases. And those who were troubled with unclean spirits were cured. And all the crowd sought to touch him, for power came out from him and healed them all.

> And he lifted up his eyes on his disciples, and said:
> "Blessed are you who are poor, for yours is the kingdom of God.
> "Blessed are you who are hungry now, for you shall be satisfied.
> "Blessed are you who weep now, for you shall laugh.
> "Blessed are you when people hate you and when they exclude you and revile you and spurn your name as evil, on account of the Son of Man! Rejoice in that day, and leap for joy, for behold, your reward is great in heaven; for so their fathers did to the prophets.
> "But woe to you who are rich, for you have received your consolation.
> "Woe to you who are full now, for you shall be hungry.

"Woe to you who laugh now, for you shall mourn and weep.

"Woe to you, when all people speak well of you, for so their fathers did to the false prophets. (Luke 6:17-26)

Where the Heart Is

Here Jesus tells his followers that "blessed are you who are poor for yours is the kingdom of God . . . because great is your reward in heaven." This assumes an eternal perspective in this present life. Christ goes on to say, "but woe to you who are rich, for you have already been comforted." Notice he doesn't say woe to the greedy or woe to the selfish but woe to the rich. The implication is that if I am rich while others are poor and hungry, I am greedy, selfish, or blind. I become like the Pharisees who honor the Messiah with their creeds, confessions, affirmations, and worship services even though their hearts are far from him.

> The Pharisees, who were lovers of money, heard all these things, and they ridiculed him. And he said to them, "You are those who justify yourselves before men, but God knows your hearts. For what is exalted among men is an abomination in the sight of God. (Luke 16:14-15)

The Pharisees, who loved money, heard all this and were sneering at Jesus. The description is not incidental—the Pharisees loved money. This description follows the Pharisees' digestion of Jesus' parable of the shrewd manager:

> Whoever can be trusted with very little can also be trusted with much and whoever is dishonest with very little will also be dishonest with much. So if you have not been trustworthy in handling worldly wealth, who will trust you with true riches? And if you have not been trustworthy with someone else's property, who will give you property of your own? No servant can serve two masters. Either he will hate the one and love the other or he will be devoted to one and

despise the other. You cannot serve both God and money.
(Luke 16:10-13)

Then Jesus informed these sneering, money-loving Pharisees, "you are the ones who justify yourself in the eyes of men, but God knows your hearts. What is highly valued among men is detestable in God's sight" (Luke 16:15).

I'll leave it to the reader to determine what it is exactly that is so highly valued by men yet detestable to God.

> And he called the twelve together and gave them power and authority over all demons and to cure diseases, and he sent them out to proclaim the kingdom of God and to heal. And he said to them, "Take nothing for your journey, no staff, nor bag, nor bread, nor money; and do not have two tunics. And whatever house you enter, stay there, and from there depart. And wherever they do not receive you, when you leave that town shake off the dust from your feet as a testimony against them." And they departed and went through the villages, preaching the gospel and healing everywhere. (Luke 9:1-6)

Here is an account of Jesus gathering his disciples in preparation for ministry. He gave them power and authority over demons and disease and sent them to preach the kingdom of God. For some reason he told them to take nothing for the journey—no staff, no bag, no bread, no money, no extra tunic, no extra underwear, no trail mix, no credit card. Why? Was it because Jesus was mean? Masochistic? The answer may be that Spirit-empowered ministry requires such single-mindedness that anything extra—even a little spending money—would be a distraction and would mean something other than ultimate reliance on God for provision and protection. We need to ask ourselves, "What do we trust God for that we can't manufacture with our own bank accounts?"

In Luke 10, similar instructions are given to seventy-two disciples along with the warning, "I am sending you out like lambs among wolves" (Luke 10:3). While truthful, it is not the most comforting commission.

Mutually Exclusive

We really can trust God to provide our material needs for survival; the problem is we expect God to fulfill our wants for affluence, comfort, and independence. Most of us in this society are not struggling for survival but for comfort and the maintenance of our lifestyles. Perhaps it's time for affluent Christians to adopt different lifestyles. God will give food, clothing, shelter, safety, and ultimate security. Jesus' own words in Luke 12:4-5 tell us, "I tell you, my friends, do not fear those who kill the body, and after that have nothing more that they can do. But I will warn you whom to fear: fear him who, after he has killed, has authority to cast into hell. Yes, I tell you, fear him!"

Is God harsh? He can be, but he is also loving and aware of our life in every detail. We are valuable to him, but his is an eternal perspective. What's the point of storing up riches in this world and not being rich toward God? (Luke 12:21) Yes, these may be mutually exclusive pursuits (Luke 16:13). Instead, I am not to worry about this life (Luke 12). Remember, the worries of this life choke my faith (Luke 8:14). In fact, those with no faith worry about what they will eat and drink (Luke 12:30). Fear and worry paralyze our ability to act on our faith, but we don't need to be afraid. God has given us the kingdom. So sell your possessions (yes, it's there again—Luke 12:33) and give to the poor because where your treasure is is where your heart will be.

What a stark contrast between these first followers who were called to ministry and our own experience. It's hard to talk about radical nonmaterialism without appearing harsh, critical, and legalistic. This is not my intent, but an honest comparison of my own experience and that described in Scripture leaves me unsatisfied with my own obedience. I find myself wondering about Christians who spend millions of dollars on buildings to honor one who told us he does not dwell in temples made with hands. There is something incongruous about a church in which people sit in cushioned pews in sanctuaries with sunlight pouring through stained glass windows, listening to clergy through thousand-dollar sound systems and reading from gilded copies of the Bible. Jesus said, "[I]f any man would come after me, let him deny himself." It is one thing to love the wretched of the earth so much that you would be willing to sacrifice everything for them, but it is quite another thing to actually quit your high-paying job and move downward so you can better serve those around you. Being willing if called by God and actually doing it are worlds apart; we may be willing, but are we ready?

We Trust God with Our Souls but Not Our Lives

A pastor friend of mine explained to me that his denomination has solid financial commitment to its pastors in order to free them from financial worries and allow them to focus totally on their ministry. I must ask, however, am I truly freed from the worries of this life as I accumulate more wealth, more stuff, a pay raise, and financial security, or do I actually free myself from the worries of this life by rejecting the accumulation mindset of my society? Are my assets my God, or is God my God? Can I trust God enough to not only surrender to him my rhetoric, my will, my family, my wealth, my security, and my positions, knowing he will provide and also knowing sometimes God lets us linger in want? Will I then allow him to totally transform my mind and desires through his spirit so they conform to his will and let him empower me by his spirit to be used in ways beyond what I could ask or think?

The irony, of course, is that such radical surrender brings freedom, not slavery. A play depicts the life of Thomas Becket, a libertine who enjoys a life of debauchery and hedonism with his closest friend, the king of England. However, Becket finds himself appointed archbishop of Canterbury, placed in this lofty position of church leadership by the king, who wanted the spokesperson for the church to be a man who wouldn't criticize his excessive ways. After being invested with the responsibility of spiritual leadership, Becket is completely transformed. Just before his ordination as archbishop, he gathers the poor into the sanctuary and gives them his earthly possessions. As he moves among them, giving away his clothing and jewelry, he abruptly stops, turns to the front of the church, and waving his fists at the crucified Jesus on the cross he screams, "You! You are the only one who knows how easy this is!"

Becket had discovered the radical nonmaterialism and surrender to Christ that brings freedom, joy, and personal transformation. He burned with a passion for God rather than things, and in this irresponsible selflessness he was faithful in the little things, so God gave him bigger things and empowered him through the Holy Spirit to participate in life-changing ministry.

But we must not forget that this life-changing freedom brought about by allegiance to God also brought about his death. When he had caused enough trouble for the king, the king let it be known he wished for someone to end this troublesome man's life. Becket, killed by four knights as he entered evening worship, died for his belief, because of his belief.

There are people who really hunger for such an upside-down value system. Teenagers identify with punk-rock culture because it reflects rejection of our culture's wealth and affluence. They recognize the shallowness of material pursuits, especially after having grown up watching Mom and Dad chase the American dream only to end up unfulfilled and out of breath. "This is radical Christianity?" they ask. The irony is that youth culture identifies more with hero bands epitomizing rebellion against the status quo than with Jesus Christ who makes the social rebellion of these young radicals look like nothing more than crossing the street against the Don't Walk sign.

By the Difference It Will Make

I had a conversation with Michael, a college sophomore who'd purchased a new stereo right around the time I'd bought a relatively new car. After admiring each other's good taste, we contemplated the repercussions of selling our possessions and giving the money to feed people, clothe people, or do whatever else we felt God leading us to do with it. The more we talked, the more enthusiastic Michael got. "I could do that!" he exclaimed. "I could sell my stereo and just use yours. I don't really need it." I could see his wheels spinning. "In fact," he said, "I'd love to be part of a church that challenged me to sell my stereo and take some of these ideas we've been talking about seriously." It was a pretty extensive system, and Michael's love of music was reflected in the thousand and one CDs cluttering his bedroom.

As we continued to talk, Michael observed that no one else he knew would think about selling a stereo and giving the money away, not even friends who claimed to be Christians. He'd be the only one.

"Maybe at first," I said, "but perhaps someone has to start. Someone has to be the first. It's like dominos. The first one has to fall down in order to get the chain falling. Perhaps obedience begins through one person's act of faith."

"Yeah" acknowledged Michael, "but what would probably happen is that I would fall over and find out I'm too far from the second domino to knock it over. So there I am, lying on my back, alone, and without a stereo."

"You don't live in close enough community with anyone to have that domino effect," I replied. "The church isn't really the church, and you do not exist as the church with anyone—you're an individual."

Michael kept his stereo, and I drove that car until it died, and the American Church still exists as an individualistic body mostly void of the intimacy, community, self-sacrifice, and the Holy Spirit-empowerment described in Scripture and longed for in the hearts of Christ's people. We have not been faithful with the little things, and we have failed to be a community that truly enables its people to live by our convictions. Usually the result is compromised convictions: "If I can't live by them, I might as well change them." We maintain our intellectual, detached convictions in our thinking but don't change our actions or infringe on the practicality of our lifestyles. Thus we conform to the image of the world and submit the Scripture to our own experience and desires, all the while going about the business of "church" pursuits, programs, and politics.

Break Out the Rollers—Brushes Aren't Big Enough

The church is no longer the Church (there, I've said it again). Of course I'm talking about the institution of church in our culture, and although I hesitate to paint with broad strokes the landscape of church existence, I feel some clarification is in order regarding the nature of the church universal and the practice of the church locally.

Somewhere along the way the New Testament church has been lost. What started as a radical movement, a revolution empowered by God through the Holy Spirit, has become a static institution. Many churches buzz with outer-circle activity but lack inner-circle reality. The grassroots movement of Acts, characterized by changed lives and dynamic witness, has become the board meetings of organized religion characterized by budget reports and books of Church Order interpretations. Is it unavoidable that over time a dynamic movement becomes stagnant? Is it even possible for the church to exist as a living, breathing organism, the body of Christ? What has happened?

A revolution begins with a grassroots movement characterized by a fresh movement of God in the hearts of individuals, a commitment to prayer and Scripture, and a new openness to God's vision for his people. Out of such a movement emerges leadership that gives shape and direction to the movement. Over time the movement becomes organized. Structures and strategies are put in place, documents and manuals are developed to teach and direct new members of the movements and activities of the infant organization, and the organization eventually becomes institutionalized. At this point the structures, strategies, policies, and programs become sacred. The fresh movement of God's spirit in people's hearts and dependence on God's power to change lives is replaced with the stagnation of formality in people's stomachs and a dependence on institutional programming for the organization's survival. The revolution is over; the last phase is decline and death.

To some extent this is the phenomena of denominations through the years. God began revivals through grassroots movements, but over time revolutions became institutionalized and died.

In my religion classes at college we learned about differences in religious movements that can be applied to the New Testament church of Acts and the institutional church of the modern era. One can be seen as a sect, the other as an ecclesia. The sect of the New Testament church required a changed life and pledge of allegiance for membership. A sect is characterized by a certain amount of intolerance for those who refuse to sell out to the essentials of the sect (Ananias and Sapphira). A person joins a sect by being converted, but, membership in an ecclesia happens primarily though birth or socialization. The sense of conversion is lost, as is the adherence to certain unalterable essentials. With the absence of conversion and selfless commitment, the dynamism of the sect fades into tolerance and a self-serving club mentality. The club erects a building (or clubhouse), institutes policy, and creates programs and secret handshakes. The package is mistakenly labeled "church."

A church near my house holds 1,200 for each service, but how many people do they help? How many people have gotten out of those seats and gone into the world to be the presence of God in the world today to be the church? So often in today's world church has become a spectator sport; we go, we watch, and if our team does well we cheer and come back next week. If our team falters, we complain and decide if we need to replace members of the team or jump ship to another team. We tend to place significance on the number of people we reach each week and not the number of people in whose lives we have made a difference. The church has become stagnant in so many ways. If we are great at missions, they are always in another country, and the people two doors down from the church get ignored and neglected. If we are good at taking care of our own, we neglect the needs of the church universal. But often we don't reach out to the world at large and completely ignore the person two doors down. We tend to take care of our own, but only on Sunday mornings and Wednesday nights. We need to be about dismantling the institutional church. We need to be about seeking out the greater community, be it two doors down or an ocean away, and growing and seeking beyond our own front door. We shouldn't be worried about how many people we draw each Sunday; we should be focusing on how many people are going out from our doors to reach others who haven't heard about the love of Christ. We should be bragging on how we are so busy in the community we don't need to add on; we're out on the front lines, not in our building.

The church assembled and the church dispersed are both the church, but the church dispersed is in tragic disarray. Too often buildings and programs have become thieves who rob the church of vitality and bring on spiritual stagnation not through laziness or lack of effort but by demanding so much time and energy for nonessential, outer-circle pursuits. We eventually move away from the inner-circle experience that gave us a vision and a purpose and began a spiritual revolution in our lives in the first place.

Locks that Break

When the church builds greater facilities and elevates its programs to the status of a sacred call, when programs become an end rather than a means to an end, this creates an artificial need to constantly validate the existence of the buildings and the programs. This is a dangerous trap that often results in an attempt to squeeze God's radical vision for the church into what already exists and is already being done. The outer circle rather than God in the center becomes our pursuit. The institution lives, but the revolution dies.

The church must be about offensive penetration rather than defensive reinforcement. The church must never recline on the couch of internal maintenance and self-complacency. Too often the church becomes an institution led by professionals whose main job seems to be to keep the institution functioning smoothly while producing people who are as happy, comfortable, and fulfilled as possible. The internal focus is both a by-product and contributing factor of our stagnation.

Let me remind you what Jesus proclaims about the fire we will face. In Matthew chapter 16, Peter confesses Jesus as Lord. Jesus states, "And I tell you, you are Peter, and on this rock I will build my church, and the gates of hell shall not prevail against it." As a new Christian, I was taught that the interpretation of this passage was that Peter's confession, not Peter himself, was the rock that Jesus' church would be built upon. I still find that interpretation credible. "[A]nd the gates of hell shall not prevail against it" was always taught to mean that in the kingdom of God you were safe from hell and all the evil that it brought against people; that in this kingdom hell could not come through. But as I've done more studying, I've become aware of a new theory. This is not uniquely my own; it's been influenced by many theologians' thoughts on God's kingdom. I don't believe Jesus was saying that evil could not get into the gates of heaven. In fact, if Job is any illustration at all, Satan easily walks into the gates of heaven. But I believe this statement is much more dangerous than any Christian I grew up with ever realized.

The gates of hell not prevailing are not our gates being safe from evil. It is evil not being able to hold back Jesus and his followers who descend into hell to spread the message of the saving grace of Jesus. We are not to remain safe in our little magical kingdom and sing songs in white terry-cloth robes; we are to go through the gates of hell with the message of Christ, and even the gates of hell will not be able to stop us. The gates of evil, which attempt to repel anything worthy, honorable, and godly, will not be able to stop people dedicated to sharing the good news of Jesus Christ. The church is not here so we can be safe; the church was built to be a battering ram brought to bear on the gates of hell.

For the Want of a Hose

Kierkegaard tells the story of a small-town fire chief (*Attack Upon Christendom,* 1854-1855, p. 193). Things went well for the chief for quite some time as he worked on the fire department's readiness and effectiveness in case a fire ever broke out. The townspeople grew to love the chief and appreciated his efforts. He usually had the courtesy to stop and chat, and he always had the time to smile and play with the children as they passed by the station. Everyone agreed he was a good influence in the community; they bragged about what a good fire chief they had.

Then one day a fire broke out in one of the busier sections of town. By the time the chief and his crew arrived on the scene, the fire was a blazing inferno. To the chief's surprise, townspeople had gathered near the burning building armed with pails, pitchers, squirt guns, and smiles. "What's going on here?" the fire chief screamed as he tried to move his vehicles and equipment through the crowd. "Well, captain," replied an onlooker busy squirting his water pistol toward the blaze, "we want you to know how much we appreciate you being here in our community (*squirt, squirt*). We want to support and encourage you in any way we can (*squirt, squirt*) and even though we may not be able to do much, we want you to know we're behind you all the way" (*squirt, squirt*). "Get the hell out of here!" yelled the normally cordial fire chief. "This is no place for uncommitted people armed with squirt guns. This is a dangerous place, and only those willing to give their lives belong here. Move! You're in the way."

Is the fire chief out of line? Is he being rude, insensitive, or even intolerant? The obvious answer is yes he is. But just as obvious is the appropriateness of his response. The fire chief cared deeply for the people of the town, but in this case their lack of commitment was a hindrance and a danger.

In Kierkegaard's story, the fire chief tells the police chief that if the people won't go peacefully, beat them away. The people were only trying to help. It's not easy putting out a fire with squirt guns, but they were diligently trying. Why did the chief consider that a bad thing?

Much like the church today, the townspeople wanted desperately to help, but they weren't prepared to do whatever it took to put out the fire. They were happy to shoot squirt guns and throw pitchers of water at the fire and look around to see what a great job each other was doing, and they were keeping very busy at it. It didn't matter to them that they were not being effective, that they were losing the battle and also hindering those people who could really put out the fire. They wanted to feel important and needed even if they weren't.

There is always a fine line between legalism and tolerance, both of which are sinful, inappropriate responses to the grace of God.

Boldly Go

To rest while living in the center is one of the most difficult things to do. At the outside of the circle is a great deal of activity; the world is abuzz with activity. At the center, everything is very still. At the center, time seems to stop. At the center, God is in control. All the programs, evangelistic opportunities, and plans take a backseat to God's agenda. The outer rings of the circle don't stop moving or cease to be, but the center is where everything comes from and begins. Without the center nothing else can really be rotating or moving at all. It is from the center that everything comes and gains momentum. We need to get to the center so we can effectively go out. Only from the center will we ever truly be able to impact those living on the outside. Only from the center will we be able to guide our course and not just be swept up in the fray.

Inside Out

At the center there is community, you and the trinity of God. As we move out in each situation there is or better put there should be community. We are not called to live and work alone. We are not called to be the solitary figure standing on the mountain top looking over all we have conquered. We are called to humbly go as God calls with those he has called and together bring the message of Jesus: Repent for the Kingdom of God is at hand. We are to go in community and to bring community in as we go.

We are to start with the Father, Son and Holy Spirit and build from there. We are to go together and gather. We are to recruit and grow. We are to be insula. God works through individuals who gather together to accomplish his will. God always starts the call. It's up to us if we are willing to respond.

ABOUT THE AUTHOR

Bruce M. Snoap II has a couple of academic letters after his name, but the best titles he carries are those of husband, father, and friend. Like most people who come from a normal life filled with amazing things, he's discovered that life is meant to be shared.

While we all know what "community" means, it looks different for each of us. The community that Bruce currently resides with is in Michigan. He lives with his bride, four children, two frogs and a dog. He is part of a dynamic, growing community actively seeking to be more like Christ.